THE CONSUMER PLAYBOOK

by Mauree Miller

Illustrations by Paula Hewitt Amram

Consumerplaybook@gmail.com
www.consumerplaybook.com

Copyright © 2014 Mauree Miller
All rights reserved.

ISBN: 1503136574
ISBN 13: 9781503136571
Library of Congress Control Number: 2014920306
CreateSpace Independent Publishing Platform
North Charleston, South Carolina

For Howard. For so many reasons…

TABLE OF CONTENTS

PROLOGUE: WHY IS THERE A NEED TO SPEAK UP? ····· xi
IN THE BEGINNING ···································· 1
A FEW WORDS ABOUT FAMILY ························ 8
THE RULES OF THE ROAD ···························· 9

ASK AND YOU SHALL RECEIVE—
MOST OF THE TIME ································ 15
    THE RULE OF TEN ································ 17
    IT CAN'T HURT TO ASK ··························· 22
    GAUGING YOUR POSITION ························ 28

SWEATING THE SMALL STUFF ····················· 31
    YOUR MOTHER IS CHARMING BUT WHERE'S
    MY VEGETABLE? ·································· 33
    MAY I HAVE THE ENVELOPE PLEASE ············ 35
    PEANUT BUTTER AND PRIMER—A LESSON IN
    PRODUCT DESIGN ································ 37
    I'D LIKE TO SEE THE EGRESS AND YOUR
    PRICING POLICY ································· 40
    CHANGING THE SUPERMARKET TO A
    SUPER MARKET ·································· 43
    WOULD YOU LIKE YOUR TRASH PICKED UP OR
    DELIVERED? ······································ 46

CELLING YOUR SOUL · 49
    THE CELL PHONE GAME · 51
    HARDWARE OR HARD WEAR? · 54
    THE EXTRA TERRESTRIAL PHONE ON
    LIFE SUPPORT · 59

SMALL BUSINESSES/BIG PROBLEMS · · · · · · · · · · · · · · · 61
    BEJEWELDED AND BE SCREWED · · · · · · · · · · · · · · · · · · · 63
    SOMETHING'S FISHY · 69
    GRILL OF MY DREAMS · 73
    BURIED ALIVE · 75

TRUE STORIES I COULDN'T POSSIBLY MAKE UP · · 79
    NEVER CLEAN YOUR SUNGLASSES WITH NAIL
    POLISH REMOVER—A MANAGER HORROR STORY · · 81
    I'M NOT A BANK ROBBER—HOW I ALMOST GOT
    ARRESTED WHEN I TRIED TO DEPOSIT MONEY
    IN THE BANK · 85

MORE MANAGER TRICKS · 89
    DRESSING UP · 91
    THE PHANTOM NIGHT MANAGER · · · · · · · · · · · · · · · · 96

I DON'T KNOW WHY ANYONE WOULD WANT TO SKIN A CAT BUT THERE'S MORE THAN ONE WAY TO DO IT · 99
    BUTTON UP AND MAKE IT SNAPPY · · · · · · · · · · · · · · · 101
    FROM REFRIGERATOR TO TOILET—A TALE OF
    HOME REPAIR · 106

EXPERT OR MYTH? · 115
    CONVERSATIONS WITH MY CAR · · · · · · · · · · · · · · · 117
    EXPERT OR NOT · 121

TABLE OF CONTENTS

CORPORATE GIANTS—HOW TO CLIMB THE BEANSTALK · · · 129
    MORTGAGE SLEIGHT OF HAND · · · 133
    CABLE WARS—THE SHOT IN THE FOOT · · · 139
    FLYING UNDER THE RADAR · · · 143
    WE COUNT—YOU DON'T · · · 151

RELATIONSHIPS—THEY LOVE ME/ THEY LOVE ME NOT · · · 153
    IF YOU WON'T TAKE MY CALLS, I'LL FIND YOU ANYWAY · · · 155
    WINDOWS OF TIME AND HOW TO CLOSE THEM · · · 159
    DON'T BE TAKEN FOR GRANTED · · · 161

WITH STRINGS ATTACHED: PERKS—HOW TO MAKE THE MOST OF THEM · · · 165
    REBATE CARDS–FIGURING OUT THE PUZZLE · · · 167
    PROMOTION OR CONFUSION–GETTING THE BEST PRICE · · · 173

CUSTOMER SERVICE—THE INS AND OUTS · · · 179
    PUTTING HOSPITABLE BACK INTO THE HOSPITALITY INDUSTRY (THE COUPLE WHO GROWS TOGETHER ADVOCATES TOGETHER) · · · 181
    DON'T SPEAK IN BUREAUCRATESE AND DON'T CALL ME MA'AM · · · 185
    THESE BOOTS ARE MADE FOR SHOPPING · · · 188
    SHOWDOWN IN THE MEN'S DEPARTMENT · · · 192
    CALL CENTERS–DON'T CALL US · · · 197
    FOREIGN TERRITORY · · · 200

HEALTHCARE—THE CHALLENGES OF DEALING WITH A WORLD OF ITS OWN ·······················**205**
    THE CASE OF THE DEAD DOCTOR ················ 213
    HIDDEN PROVIDERS ································ 217
    MAXIMIZING YOUR INSURANCE COVERAGE ····· 222
    A FEW WORDS TO THE WISE ······················ 231

KEEPING THE MOMENTUM GOING ················**234**

ACKNOWLEDGMENTS ······························**237**

This work is based on real events. Other than the names of the author, her husband, and her children, names of individuals with whom the author interacted have been changed to protect the identity of those involved.

PROLOGUE: WHY IS THERE A NEED TO SPEAK UP?

My husband and I were staying in a hotel that had been beautifully renovated. Everything was lovely—with the exception of the restaurant. What had formerly been a spacious room with a central and accessible buffet had been redone as an attractive but small space.

We went to breakfast and saw what looked like an army of people sitting outside of the restaurant. Not one of them looked happy. We had to wait about ten minutes just to get our name on the list, and then we were told that the wait would be about fifteen minutes. Joining the ranks of the disgruntled, we peered inside and saw quite a few empty tables. We thought to ourselves, "Why aren't people being seated? Okay, whatever"- we thought that we could wait the fifteen minutes.

After sixteen minutes, with nothing happening, we decided that I would hold our place and my husband would find a hotel manager. While on that quest, my husband saw a very confused and stressed looking guest wandering in the lobby. My husband and Mr. Frazzled started to talk. The man was trying to find someone who would give him information about checkout time and was worried that he would be charged for an extra day because he had been delayed by the breakfast problem. He had asked a bellman, who simply said that he didn't know and walked

WHY IS THERE A NEED TO SPEAK UP?

away. This was unacceptably poor customer service. My husband politely but firmly pulled a desk clerk aside to help Mr. Frazzled, who was relieved to find that he was within timeframe for checkout. Before my husband could say anything else, the man thanked him and trotted away to pack.

Meanwhile, the restaurant hostess called our name. The buffet was sparse and disorganized. Annoyed, I grabbed a waiter and asked for some muffins. Not the breakfast experience that we had expected.

With the restaurant and lobby so busy, we decided to get in touch with the manager by email or phone later to let him know about the problems with the customer service and the restaurant. The goal was to have the situation rectified before our next visit.

So, what does this have to do with this book? In a nutshell, I am writing this book because of everything that happened that morning in the hotel. My fervent hope is that there won't be a Mr. Frazzled panicked by the fear of being charged for an extra day in the hotel when he had been waylaid by breakfast chaos. Instead, he'll receive good customer service to address his concerns. He will be able to speak up and explain that the hotel's disorganized restaurant had delayed him, so any overtime would be the hotel's responsibility and should not be charged to him.

People would not be sitting around the lobby waiting for breakfast. Instead, they will know how to get to managers to get the place running properly. Better yet, the restaurant will be running smoothly based on management action in response to customer feedback. In other words, I want to give you the tools to speak up, to address poor customer service and management, and to learn that you have the power to get problems fixed rather than feeling like a victim.

If you speak up, things can change. I can prove it—just read this book.

IN THE BEGINNING

James Cagney was a wonderful actor, well known for his portrayals of gangsters in the 1930s. Off screen, he was equally recognized for his grit and for latching on to causes that were important to him and to his fellow actors. An early member of the Screen Actor's Guild, he was known for fighting the powerful movie studios and for being among the first to successfully challenge the tight control of the studios and their powerful leaders. Pugnacious and effective, Cagney was labeled a Professional Againster by Jack Warner, the head of Warner Studios. I am a Professional Againster. It doesn't always make me the most popular girl on the block, but I am effective. Over the years, I've honed my skills, and I can get things done. I have even learned to find ways of making allies and friends of many of the people on the opposite side of my issue. Although I come by all of this honestly and naturally, I have found that it is important to find ways of doing things by adapting to the situation. I used to resign myself to the fact that some people will grit their teeth when they see me coming—and that's okay. But, I've also found that I can be charming and end a situation with a smile rather than a blood bath. However, there are times when I do leave a trail of wounded along the road.

I work as a Consumer Advocate, but I also live as one. I now work in healthcare advocacy, although I am trained as a psychologist and have always been a writer. A basic understanding of what makes people tick and the ability to communicate are critical in being an effective Againster. But, as you will see, I pull whatever works out of my consumer toolbox to make things happen.

Over the years, I have battled and negotiated, begged and wheedled, pushed and banged, until I could achieve the goal of making rational things happen in an irrational world. In the process, I found that what I had always believed was so true—that my writing and speaking experience, my psychologist's ability to assess people, and my personality all added up to effectiveness. Even if you don't have this background, you can find your own skills to be effective. Think about the times when you've achieved a difficult goal, or when you have wanted to do that, but haven't quite been able to get there. By taking inventory of these situations, you can begin to develop your own consumer toolbox.

I started very young. When I was five, I had my tonsils removed. My father was a doctor at the hospital where the surgery was done. Irritable and impatient, I was ready to go home quickly. A nurse said to me "You can't leave until you take this medicine." I remember glaring at her, climbing up to stand on the bed (all three and a half feet of me), putting my hands on my hips, shaking my curls, and saying in my best five year old authoritative tone, "My daddy's a doctor here, and I don't have to do anything I don't want to do." Obnoxious—yes. Effective—no. Much to my dismay, my father walked in and said, "Mauree, you can't go home until you take this medicine."

At that point in time, whether instinctive, or learned from observation, I had the basic principles right. Back then, the execution was wrong. Body language is important. Somehow, I must have known that my five year old height and a mild-mannered demeanor weren't going to do it, so I instinctively climbed onto the bed. At least then I could look the nurse in the eye—or almost in the eye. My facial expression said that I meant business.

Who you know is important, so invoking my father's status seemed to be the right thing to do. What I didn't realize was that no adult was going to take a five year old seriously, especially when I didn't hold any cards. There would be no advantage for the nurse to do what I asked and no consequence for her to ignore me. I had no leverage.

Over the years, I've come to use the basic principles of my youthful attempt at being effective, but polished the skill and also gained some stature. (I mean that figuratively—I'm still short.)

I learned from the best. My parents were effective people and I could watch them as they made things happen. My mother, Belle, was a lieutenant in the Army during World War II. She certainly could bark a good command, but she was also charming and managed to accomplish her goal with her charm most of the time. But when she was icy, you could see the freeze in the air. My father, George, could be tough when he needed to get something done. I watched his language, his glare, the tone of his voice. The Belle bark and the George glare could melt concrete, but the Belle charm could melt concrete just as well. Style has its place. You need to know your style and adapt it to the situation.

My sister, Ellen, took her cues from the charm end. When she had her tonsils out, I overheard my mother talking about how the nurses thought that she was so cute and how they loved to play with her. I guess that at age five, cute was better than imperious. So, I learned. But, as time went on, I found that being more forceful could also work. Besides, I wasn't very good at being cute anyway.

You need to look at your strengths—are you charming? Are you forceful? Can you communicate well? You can use what comes naturally and add the other pieces with time and practice.

IN THE BEGINNING

I took my cues from the tough angle, but I learned to incorporate some grace. Watching my father taught me most of what I know. Practice over time refined the skill. To this day, although I have been a Professional Againster for years, my father's words stay with me.

The piano issue was one of my first important lessons. My mother and my piano teacher went to the local department store to buy a new piano. The piano arrived, but there was a problem. After a few unsuccessful attempts to go through the piano department to fix the problem, my father went to the president of the store. Very quickly, the old piano was replaced with a new one. My father's comment—"When you can't get satisfaction at the bottom, go straight to the top." He was right then, and most of the time, it works. You have to periodically adjust what the top means—it could mean a savvy salesperson, a supervisor, or the CEO of the company. It all depends on who has the vision and the power to make things right.

Presentation is critical. I listened to my father's choice of words. He was clear. His words were carefully chosen. Even when he didn't personally know his opponent, he *knew* his opponent. The point was to know what he wanted to achieve and to find a way to figure out what would hook the guy on the opposite side into seeing his point of view.

Then there was my mother. I watched her stand straight and tall when she wanted to make a point. Her stance said: "How you look is a reflection of who you are." Remember, lawyers wear suits in court. Imagine a lawyer in khakis and a knit shirt. Would you take him or her as seriously? My daughter is a lawyer. She is petite, and her voice is the lovely modulated tone of a young twenty-something. But when she has to dress for business, her suit, her heels, the stockings, and the demeanor transform her into a professional who will be taken seriously. You don't have to wear a suit for every

5

encounter, but you need to look the part. If you are interacting only on the phone or by mail or email, you need an authoritative tone so that the person on the other side will imagine that you look the part.

When we were selling our first house, the potential buyers were difficult. We had an attorney whom we hadn't met, but who spoke with significant gravitas. All of his communication with the buyer was by phone until the settlement. When we finally met him, he looked young enough to be a college student. Thank goodness for the voice—it was the voice that got the sale accomplished on our terms.

To accomplish a goal, you have to be persistent. You have to be prepared to hang on until your objective is met or until there is nowhere else to go. If one strategy doesn't work, you need to try other strategies. And your opposition has to know that you mean business and that you're not going away.

Why continue to fight the battles? Most of the time, it seems pretty obvious—if something is wrong, you need to make it right. This is a part of the answer. The other part of the answer lies in a broader view of the world. That broader view has everything to do with what's right and the idea of a civilized world.

We can start with the basic premise that whoever has the power abuses it. While this may seem to be a cynical worldview, there is also truth here. In a civilized world, people need to be reasonable and fair and to balance the power base. Sometimes, the balance system works. Other times, it doesn't. That's where assertiveness and effectiveness come in. When the power balance is skewed, you need to re-set it. In today's world, the power imbalance can exist on a small level—the times when you, as an individual, are being shafted. At other times, it exists on a larger scale, such as when corporations use their size and power to take bigger advantage—when many people are being shafted. When you consider the power base at any given point in time, also consider the fact that creating

IN THE BEGINNING

change isn't always easy, but it is possible. If you don't try, you'll never know. How many social causes have resulted in change when people push back at what is wrong?

Joseph Welch is my hero. In the early 1950s, Senator Joseph McCarthy ruled the United States Senate. He ran Congressional hearings, looking for Communists while creating a landscape of fear as he controlled the country with his witch hunt. His power was absolute. Lives were ruined based on innuendo and fear. Joseph Welch was a lawyer who challenged McCarthy. With an intensity of purpose and his scathing words, he pushed back at McCarthy: *"Until this moment, Senator, I think I never really gauged your cruelty or your recklessness... You have done enough. Have you no sense of decency?"* These well chosen and clearly stated words brought down McCarthy. The reign of terror ended. Speaking out when few would, one man had the ultimate impact in stepping on an absolute tyrant. I aspire to be Joseph Welch every day.

My goal is usually to have a broader impact than simply winning my argument. Sometimes that happens, and sometimes it doesn't. I'll take the big wins, the smaller wins, and live with the few that don't achieve the goal. However, I usually can't let go. If something is wrong, I need to speak up. You have to decide how far you can go and how to choose your battles. The outcome can be rewarding when you win, although the process can frequently be tough. But, in looking back on my consumer adventures, I can absolutely say that going the distance is worth it.

A FEW WORDS ABOUT FAMILY

I live with my husband, Howard. We have raised two children, Cory and Tracy. All of them have picked up effective consumer tools both from watching me and by using their own individual skill sets. Howard has his own way of being effective, but he has borrowed from my consumer toolbox with nice results.

At age five, Tracy turned to me as we were walking into the mall and said: "Are we going to talk to a manager today?"

Cory hates shopping. With a twinkle in his eye, he says that he has PTSD from all of the shopping hassles that he's witnessed. Nice excuse—I know that he's seen a lot, but I also know that he's just not a shopper. That's okay as long as he makes sure that he replaces the socks with holes in them and keeps toothpaste in the house.

I've also learned from Howard and from Cory and Tracy as well. Mixing the pot is a good thing. Now we've added Jonah, Tracy's husband. Like Cory and Tracy, he has many effective ways of managing the world around him, but he has also incorporated some tips from his mother-in-law.

It feels good to be effective, but it is also rewarding to watch the family meet consumer challenges armed with my guidance and adding their own special touches.

THE RULES OF THE ROAD

There are basic principles that can make you effective. In each of the stories in this book, you will see how these principles work to achieve the result—a return, a credit, a refund, a change in policy, or addressing bad customer service. You can learn to make things right in any setting—a large corporation, a retail chain, a single owner shop, and anywhere else. Just follow my yellow brick road, and I'll take you there. I've had friends say to me, "I heard the Mauree in my head," "What would Mauree do in this situation?" or "I did a Mauree." They've heard my litany of adventures, and realize that walking away from a bad situation isn't usually the best option and what can seem hopeless really isn't if you follow the mantra.

THE RULES OF THE ROAD

What is my mantra? Eight simple principles:

1. **Stand your ground.** Never give up, even if it's a struggle to stay the course. It can be wearing—sometimes I wonder if I'm shriveling and shrinking because of the wear and tear. Maybe I am, but I'll never stop until I finish, and anyone who's dealt with me knows that.

2. **Obstacles can be overcome.** The stonewall is often an effective tool that people use when trying to avoid making things right or giving service. It is rare that you can't get past the stonewall. How often do I hear "I'm the manager" or "the manager/executive doesn't talk to people"? There is almost always a way to get up the ladder to the right person to resolve your issue.

3. **Be creative.** Sometimes the logical path to resolution isn't so obvious. If you start on the path but find yourself floundering or stymied, think creatively. Think outside of the box and consider creative and less obvious ways to approach an argument. Sometimes it may be a bit of a challenge, but you can go off path to get back on track.

4. **Be clear on the problem and state it succinctly.** You can't get your point across if you don't know what you're talking about. Make sure that you are on solid ground before you begin, and tell your story clearly and articulately.

5. **Escalate.** If you aren't making progress at the lower levels—the cashier, the salesperson, the customer service representative—go higher. There are two basic criteria for escalation: 1) You aren't getting the correct result at the lower level, or 2) The situation is so complicated that someone at the lower level wouldn't be able to resolve it through standard channels.

6. **Keep good records.** When you are dealing with a difficult person, get their name so that you can pinpoint the source of the problem. If you have details, the problem person can be educated on the right approach so that things can change after you escalate the situation. When you get to the person who can resolve the issue, keep this name and contact information because you don't know when you might need to go back to him or her for follow up or for a subsequent issue. I have sometimes needed to go back to a contact and found that the person is no longer with the company. But because I have that original phone number, I can usually find the current person in the same position. When you are on the phone at the first level, not only do you need the first name of the representative, you need the last name or initial or employee ID number and the Call Center location. Armed with detail, if you later find that you were given misinformation or whatever you were trying to achieve didn't happen, you can say "I spoke to Mary X in your Houston Call Center on January 4 and she told me..." It makes it easier for the next person to see the call documentation and problem, and it gives you instant credibility. In the movie, *You've Got Mail*, Meg Ryan complains that people only use their first names, making it sound like our world is turning into "an entire generation of cocktail waitresses." We need cocktail waitresses, but not in Customer Service. I am always floored that Customer Service representatives are allowed to hide in virtual anonymity. However, I have learned to get around this minor obstacle.

7. **Make sure that you're on solid ground and have a good, logical argument.** Just because you want something doesn't mean that what you want is right. Think through the issue, put together a logical argument, and if it makes sense, go for it. If it doesn't, then just move on.

8. **The most important thing to remember—*if no one speaks up, nothing changes!***

You will see these rules repeated throughout the stories in this book. They are the foundation for effective consumerism.

ASK AND YOU SHALL RECEIVE—MOST OF THE TIME

THE RULE OF TEN

Cory has been diligent about routine car maintenance. So when he went to the car dealership for a routine oil change, he expected a simple oil change with a bill of about $40. Just after dropping the car off, the dealership called to tell him that he needed about $700 worth of work on his car. Surprise!

Cory has many talents. Understanding technical auto problems is not one of them. He comes by this honestly—I'm pretty bad on this type of issue. I always defer to Howard on cars. This started when we were first married. Like the time when a fuse blew and I thought that we needed a new car. Howard looked at me like I was crazy and 50 cents later we were good to go.

Setting aside his lack of expertise on cars, Cory has developed expertise at being an astute consumer. An unexpected $700 charge warrants questioning—big time. When he spoke with the specialist, he heard a litany of problems. Some of them made sense; others didn't. His approach:

1. He asked the specialist which were essential services, and which were overkill. The answer to that reduced the number of services and the pricing, but he still needed significant work.

2. Cory asked for an explanation of the work that was necessary in terms that a layperson could understand so that he could make an informed decision.

3. He asked for the best price on the service. The specialist gave him 10% off.

4. Cory knew that 10% wasn't much of a discount. Rule of thumb—10% is generally a minor concession. In most cases, you can achieve more if this minimal discount is so readily tossed at you. 10% is a toss out, a standard ace in the hole. So, go for more. Cory asked for a better price. The specialist said that he couldn't do that.

5. Cory asked for the manager. *When negotiation ends at the front line, go up the chain as far as you have to go until you get a better result.*

ASK AND YOU SHALL RECEIVE—MOST OF THE TIME

6. He asked the manager for a better discount and an explanation of why the charges were so high. The manager explained that the charges were high because they were in a high income part of the city. Cory lived at the very outer edge of a high income area and didn't fall into the high income classification. That is irrelevant. Where he lives, whether he's just starting his life, or whether he's a millionaire shouldn't affect the charge. However, unfortunately and unfairly, location often does determine the cost of services. This is still unacceptable. Charges should be based on the cost of the service rather than on the service location. Sometimes you can't do much about it, but sometimes you can. Cory did something about it. He used the manager's specious explanation to his advantage. He politely told him that this made no sense and wasn't making him a happy customer. And he could look for other service options if he couldn't obtain a reasonable price. The manager reduced the price by 20%. When there are other choices for goods and services, make sure that you remind the vendor of that. The vendor needs to recognize that you can go elsewhere and that if he isn't reasonable, you will do just that. And he will lose business as a result. Reasonable charges are income to a business, while $0 is lost income to the dealer if you go elsewhere.

After a quote of $700, Cory got the bill down to around $400 for necessary services only, plus a discount.

A few weeks after the car service, he received a call from the survey firm hired by the manufacturer to check service satisfaction. He explained what happened. A few days later, he received a call from the Sales Manager at the dealership. Notice I said Sales Manager. This is where the power lies—it was Sales that was charged with the responsibility of retaining customers. The Sales Manager told Cory that he hadn't realized that he was so dissatisfied. Cory was very frank about his annoyance. The Sales Manager asked Cory to let him know when he was scheduling his next service so that he could give him a free oil change and detailing service. Don't ignore service surveys. They are there for a reason. *If no one knows that there is a problem, it will never get fixed. If they do know, not only can it be fixed, it can lessen your costs for the future and build relationships within a company for future needs.* Cory now has the connection to the Sales Manager, and the dealership knows that he's not a pushover.

Cory was very pleased. He had eliminated unnecessary services and negotiated a better price for the services he really needed. He didn't ignore the follow up survey and got results from that effort. By the way, when there is not a survey, you can go to Corporate Headquarters for the company, and let them know you are having a problem. Most of the time, they will be responsive in a similar way to what Cory experienced.

Even if you're not an expert on the matter at hand, question, negotiate, and escalate.

A few months later, it was Howard's turn for an oil change at a different dealership. When he took his car in, the Service associate told him that he needed rear brakes and a few other repairs. When he picked up the car, the bill was a whopping $800 and change. Howard had the good sense to tell the dealership that the charge was too high. They immediately took off 10%.

Howard understands car technology, so that there wasn't an issue about necessary repairs. He also knows to negotiate. But, he had forgotten THE RULE OF TEN.

Howard is assertive, but he was also tired at the end of the long day. However, I wasn't tired and, of course, I am also assertive. I called the dealership and asked for the Service

Manager. I explained that Howard was given a 10% discount, but that this was insufficient. The manager asked if we had a coupon. I told him that we get all kinds of emails and mailings and I wasn't sure. His response was that the only coupon out there at that time was a 10% coupon. My reply was polite but firm: "I'm not talking about a coupon. Ten percent is a standard discount, you charge high, we're on our second car purchased from your dealership, and you can do better."

"Let me check the work order and I'll call you back," he replied. In five minutes, I got the call. He reviewed further discounts, which amounted to an additional 10%.

Remember the Rule of Ten—it really works.

IT CAN'T HURT TO ASK

There have been many situations where you can achieve a price or service by simply asking, based on rational persuasion. Pricing can be all over the map, and you can often find the right price by negotiating with the right person. Asking for something reasonable is pretty much a no-brainer. The worst that you can experience is that someone says no—and most of the time, they say yes if you have a good reason for the request.

I went to the drugstore to buy vitamins. They were having a "But One Get One" sale. That day, they didn't have my usual size bottle for the vitamins that I needed. They only had the ginormous size. I didn't need two ginormous bottles. And the bottle was so heavy that I didn't have the strength to lift it. I guess this means that I really do need the vitamins.

ASK AND YOU SHALL RECEIVE—MOST OF THE TIME

Since the BOGO promotion translated to half price per bottle, I told the clerk that my regular size was out of stock, and asked if she would charge me half price for the bigger bottle, since there weren't two of the smaller ones. She agreed that this made sense and went to her manager to override the pricing. I had a reasonable request, and she responded appropriately. *If you don't ask, you won't achieve an outcome.* Great customer service! I told the manager and clerk that I appreciated their service. Always recognize and acknowledge excellent service—it's the kind thing to do, it goes a long way for morale, and it translates to a path for the good ones to mentor others and to do the same when they move into other settings. In other words, a path to a civilized society.

So, armed with the strength from my vitamins, I could move on to more adventures.

There is a large chain store that advertises: "We are delighted to accept competitor coupons." Notice that they don't say: "We will accept…" No, they say: "We are delighted." So why is it usually an ordeal as they scrutinize the competitor coupon as if it were written in Sanskrit, find a manager, and finally take the coupon anyway? I've pointed out that they are supposed to be delighted to accept the coupon. The staff aren't amused or convinced. I discussed this with several managers, and it has gotten smoother. One day I found a 30% coupon for an entire purchase in an email from another chain store. *Look at your email. Sometimes you'll find gold buried in the routine advertising.* Luckily for me, that transaction was smooth.

Why did I use the coupon at a competing store? This store was more conveniently located. Their prices are better, too, so that 30% off lower prices becomes even more of a bargain. I handed the clerk my manufacturer's coupons, as well as my 30% competitor coupon. My initial bill was $48.99. After the 30% off, it went down to $34.29. After my manufacturer's coupons, I had a final bill of $26.79. I saved $22.20! If I hadn't noticed the store banner and if I hadn't spoken up about the matching coupons, I would have paid much more.

I've dealt with a local jeweler who has been in my area for many years. The store is family owned, with a chief jeweler and two longtime employees.

ASK AND YOU SHALL RECEIVE—MOST OF THE TIME

Periodically, I want to have rings polished so they look like new. For white gold or platinum, this means having them lightly plated with rhodium. This process happens when they are made, but it can wear off over time. I went into the jeweler with three small rings. Longtime Employee #1 was at the counter.

"It's not worth doing," he said, adding that he would charge me $30 per ring. I decided that the charge was too much and wasn't worth it. After a few more weeks, I looked again and still felt that the rings needed to be polished, so I returned to the store. This time, I spoke with Longtime Employee #2. He told me that it would cost $20 each—$10 less per ring. I left the rings with him for re-polishing. When I returned to pick them up, the bill was $70, rather than the $60 charge that I expected. (Remember, he promised to charge me $20 each.) I reminded Employee #2 of the charge per ring that he promised me. When we finished the transaction, he charged me $30 for all three rings. Going from $90 to $30 was a good deal. If I hadn't said anything, I would have paid more. And, depending on who is working with you, the price can change.

I saw a special rate advertised for a New York hotel. Because of the rate, Howard and I decided to stay over on a Saturday night. The deal was for a junior suite. The hotel told us that we were being put in the newer area. We waited quite a while for our elevator, got up to the room, and found that the front desk had forgotten to encode our keys. We called Security for assistance. After a fifteen minute interlude while Security also waited for an elevator, we finally got into the room.

Various areas of this hotel have separate elevator banks. Howard and I found that an elevator in our wing's set had been out of service for several days. Since the hotel was busy, we shortened our stay and left earlier than planned on Sunday due to the shortage of working elevators. The bottom line here is that in a hotel this busy, it would seem that the elevator could have been addressed as an urgent issue, but no repairs were done during the weekend. The problem put a damper on what should have been a more relaxing weekend—the whole idea for the short getaway.

What to do? I called the Executive office of the hotel chain. Based on the problem, they credited our Rewards account with enough points for a free night. That was good, but when we went to book a new stay we found that the credit was for a more basic room. Since the earlier stay had been for a junior suite, I called the hotel manager, explained the problem, and asked for an upgrade on the free room since that had been the room size for the earlier problematic visit. She immediately understood and arranged a junior suite and a fruit plate on arrival.

If I didn't say anything, we'd have left with a bad taste for the hotel because of the poor elevator maintenance. By asking for a reasonable accommodation, we had a new chance at a relaxing getaway, and we'd return to the hotel based on their good faith actions.

Going through the massive number of pre-Christmas promotional emails, I found a retailer email advertising 50% off of one full priced item if the purchase was made before 1 PM.

"Hmm," I thought. "It's 10:35. Do I have time?" Of course I did!

I had ordered a sweater on a 40% off promotion a few days earlier, and hadn't received it yet. Now I saw a 50% offer. What the heck—I called Customer Service. After the representative thanked me for being a customer, I asked if they could adjust the price of the pending order. She looked at the terms—no adjustments. However, I had tried to access the terms and the website didn't give me any information, so I told the service representative that. She saw that I was

ASK AND YOU SHALL RECEIVE—MOST OF THE TIME

a longtime customer, heard my point, and agreed to make the adjustment. A legitimate request (after all, I hadn't even received the order yet), a customer friendly associate, and I got off of the phone as a satisfied customer.

GAUGING YOUR POSITION

Some time ago, Howard and I were driving a car that was one of the best we've ever owned. It was reliable, fun to drive, and good in snow. One day, we opened the mail to find a recall notice. Apparently, our car model could have a defective gas gauge. These gauges would show inaccurate levels of gasoline, and if drivers didn't keep track in some other way, they were running out of gas, with the gauge showing nowhere near "Empty".

When we received our recall, I called the dealership to arrange a replacement gauge. I was told that the replacements were on back order for six months. And that there was a waiting list of about 100 people in front of me. Six months! I'm not good at accepting what isn't reasonable. If this recall could be a safety issue—running out of gas on a highway or in the middle of nowhere —a six month backup is completely unreasonable. There had to be a better solution.

I called the 800 Customer Service line—no help. Pushing Customer Service to get me to the Corporate office, I worked my way around Corporate until I reached a Vice President. He patiently explained that there was a manufacturing delay. I patiently explained that this was unacceptable. My intent wasn't to jump the wait list, but I pointed out that if there were safety concerns, there could be manufacturer liability with a known defect and no way to fix it in a timely manner.

The VP was attentive, but couldn't do anything—or so I thought. About a week later, I received a call from my dealership, saying, "I don't know how you did it, Mrs. Miller, but we just received a gas gauge with your name on it."

Remember, it was never my intent to jump the line, but rather, to fix the problem for everyone else as well as for myself. On the other hand, if no one else could speak up to deal with the problem, I'd take the gas gauge.

SWEATING THE SMALL STUFF

YOUR MOTHER IS CHARMING BUT WHERE'S MY VEGETABLE?

Howard likes the hot turkey sandwich at our local deli. The menu was written so that it was clear to us that a salad and vegetable came with the sandwich. Under the category that included the hot turkey sandwich, the menu said: "includes soup or salad and one vegetable (unless otherwise specified)." But the waitress always interpreted the menu to read that the salad was the vegetable, which meant that the wording on the menu was ambiguous. Finally we consulted the deli manager, who agreed with the waitress. So I called the owner of the deli. He understood what I was saying and agreed that the waitress and manager were interpreting the menu incorrectly. Sweetly and humorously, he let me know that the manager was his mother.

"Your mother is charming, even if she was wrong," I responded.

In this case, Howard and I had a permanent impact on a broader scale as well. The next time we went to the deli, we found that the owner had reprinted the menus, reworded to eliminate confusion. Minor issue, lasting impact.

By the way, I learned from a lawyer friend that responsibility for ambiguity lies with the person who wrote the document. Simply put, this means that when there is ambiguity, the person who set it up has to honor the other point of view. But I wouldn't recommend suing your local deli, especially when they have the best hot turkey sandwich in town.

MAY I HAVE THE ENVELOPE PLEASE

I usually use the ATM at a mini branch of my bank. When I take cash, I like to put it in an envelope, as do many people. This branch never had envelopes available. If I asked for an envelope, the person behind the counter would generally go into a locked drawer and grudgingly hand me one. When I asked why they didn't just leave some on the counter, she responded that people  always took too many and then there were none left. I had a vision of people running around the branch with fistfuls of envelopes—doing what with them? Where were these wild-eyed envelope thieves?

Every week, I went through this little ritual, with multiple representatives telling me the same thing. Although this is a minor point, the situation just seemed silly and inconvenient for customers. I called the bank's local full service branch and asked for a Regional Manager. I called her a few times, leaving several messages, but I wasn't getting calls back. The issue was now becoming less important than the overall issue of lack of customer service. Since I was going nowhere, I called the Executive office of the bank, reached a specialist, who contacted the local Regional Manager and made sure that she got back to me. The Regional Manager apologized for her lack of responsiveness and for the situation, saying that she didn't understand why the mini-branch was putting envelopes under lock and key. She spoke with the mini branch staff, and ever since, there is always a pile of envelopes available.

While the issue is a minor one in the great landscape of life, it is nice not to have to wait in line for someone to unlock an envelope vault. But that's not the main point. The more important issue is that the Regional Manager learned that it is unacceptable not to respond to a customer, and the local employees were educated about customer service. I smile just a little bit every time I see a nice pile of envelopes on the counter, knowing that I was responsible for getting them there.

PEANUT BUTTER AND PRIMER—A LESSON IN PRODUCT DESIGN

I cut my thumb opening a plastic jar of peanut butter. Impossible, you say? No, this really happened.

There is a freshness seal under the lid of a new jar of peanut butter. It is made of a thick foil and paper material. This seems pretty safe. I'm assured that the jar was never tampered with, and freshness is guaranteed. Later, Howard pointed out that this new peanut butter tasted better than the last jar. (I have trouble figuring out when to throw things out. The old peanut butter had tasted fine and it wasn't out of date, so we used it until it was empty. I probably should have thrown it out sooner. I have lipsticks that are almost as old as my children. Rule of thumb here is that I generally throw them out when they start to smell like crayons. But, back to freshness seals.)

The peanut butter freshness seal had four microscopic tabs that should have pulled up to remove the seal. I chose one and pulled. And pulled. And pulled. I made a tiny opening, but not enough to get to the peanut butter. On to the next tab. As I pulled, it hit my thumb and I started to bleed. I held a paper towel to my thumb, and searching for a Band Aid, I found the Customer Service number on the jar and called. When I reached the representative (still bleeding), I explained what happened and suggested that they put a longer pull tab around the edge, or change the design in some way so that grabbing it would make the seal come off easily. The representative was attentive, though surprised. She hadn't heard of someone slicing their hand on the seal before, but she took the bar code information and promised to pass the problem along to their design team. She also sent me two coupons for free jars of peanut butter.

The question here is whether I'm just a klutz or whether this is a design problem that others experience but don't bother to report. Or, as my friend suggested, maybe other people use their teeth. But I'd rather have a dinged thumb than a broken tooth.

The point is that if the company never hears about the problem, there may be a lot of bloody thumbs out there. It's a minor issue, but if it's more than my klutziness, the company should change the design.

We have all seen that customer noise can create change. Remember New Coke? People protested and the old Coke was back on the shelves. When a Coca Cola spokesman said, "We're not that dumb and we're not that smart," he really summed it up—corporations often have ideas that don't sync with customer needs. If people hadn't made noise, Coca Cola would not have made the change back to the good old standard. Here, I'm making noise in the hope of avoiding future bleeding thumbs.

Then there was the primer issue. What is primer? When women get older, the makeup routine increases. Primer is like spackle; it creates a smooth surface before applying makeup. One of the first companies to develop primer had a great product in a not so great package. It came in an easy to use pump bottle. But after I used about half of the primer, the pump would stop working—press the pump and nothing came out. Most stores and cosmetic companies back their products. I returned mine to the store and they gave me a new bottle. After the same thing happened again, I returned it for a refund and changed brands. The saleswoman told me that I wasn't the only one with this problem and the company was working on a new design. My sister stayed loyal and also didn't pay for primer for about a year, returning each bottle as it stopped working. With all of the returns and reports, the company changed the design and is still a top selling brand.

I'D LIKE TO SEE THE EGRESS AND YOUR PRICING POLICY

When Cory was finishing graduate school, he needed CD holders for a project. At the big box office supply store, there were many stacks to choose from, all looking pretty much the same. Cory looked at prices and found a package that was on sale. There was a sign that said $10.99 for a package of ten with $5 off. What a good deal, especially for a graduate student on a budget.

The cashier rang up the purchase—$10.99. Where was the $5 off? Cory directed her to the Sale sign. She and Cory studied the sign for a few minutes. They finally realized that the sign was misleading. The CD holders that Cory chose were not the ones on sale, although they were placed directly behind the sign. If the customer is in a hurry and doesn't have the time to read the sign for any length of time, it's easy to scan the sign and make the logical assumption that the sign referred to the items behind it. It took too long for Cory and the cashier to figure out which were on sale. If it took that long, it was the store's problem, not Cory's.

What to do? Pay the full price or hold the store responsible for its misleading advertised special? Cory chose the latter. He politely pointed out that the sign was misleading and asked the cashier to honor the sale price. She agreed and did the right thing by taking the $5 off. This is a small issue for a small purchase, though the $5 is better in Cory's pocket. And, maybe the store will fix the sign and similar signs for the future.

It's annoying when stores do this misleading advertising thing. And they do it all the time. Are they doing it to confuse the customer, so that when a customer reaches the cash register with the non-sale item, believing it is on sale, and finds that it's not on sale, the customer takes the line of least resistance and just pays the full price for the non-sale item? (The paranoid way of looking at this issue, but possibly a valid one.) Or, maybe it's simply non-thinking or sloppy placement on the retailer's part.

I find that supermarkets are notorious for this practice. The Sale sign will be in front of the 26 ounce box of cereal, but when I go to checkout, I find that it applied to the 18 ounce box. Small print on details, wrong sign placement. What do I do? Of course, I either change the item or ask them to honor the sale price.

This situation is similar to the story of P.T. Barnum, who had a sign showing circus visitors to the "Egress". This led them to believe that there was something new and exciting to see, when "Egress" simply means exit. Barnum's goal was to have visitors leave to allow new ones to enter, and the departing visitors would have to pay again to re-enter. Not on the up and up, but very business-savvy. Signs can be powerful or misleading tools, in the past circus era and in the current marketplace.

CHANGING THE SUPERMARKET TO A SUPER MARKET

Problems at local grocery stores have been a bone of contention for me. I live in an area where there isn't much open land, so we don't get the large, nice, new supermarkets that I see in other parts of the country. When the local and much beloved department store chain, John Wanamaker, closed, part of the site was converted to a grocery store. My neighborhood hadn't seen a new grocery store in so many years that the opening of the new store required a police presence to control the traffic flow because of the sightseers who wanted to see the new store. Lacking real excitement in my neighborhood, Howard and I, along with our friends, were among the excitement challenged sightseers.

This new store was part of a local, family owned chain that had a reputation for quality and service. We had experienced this in other branches of this chain. Unfortunately, they came into our area and quickly sold to a national chain, which changed both the quality and the service. My issue was that many of the cashiers on staff were poorly trained, apathetic, and often nasty. On one occasion, I asked for paper in plastic.

"I don't have any paper," the cashier nastily replied.

"Would you mind getting some?" I politely responded.

"I'd have to walk all the way over there," she replied, pointing across the store.

At that point, I asked for the manager. He was clearly responsive and told me that he was working on customer service. Managers can act on feedback. They can't act if they don't receive the feedback. So take a moment to speak up. The result was that Nasty Cashier sees me coming and never gives me a hard time anymore. *When you are receiving poor customer service, report it. I can guarantee that if you experience it, so do others. And it won't get any better unless it's recognized and addressed.*

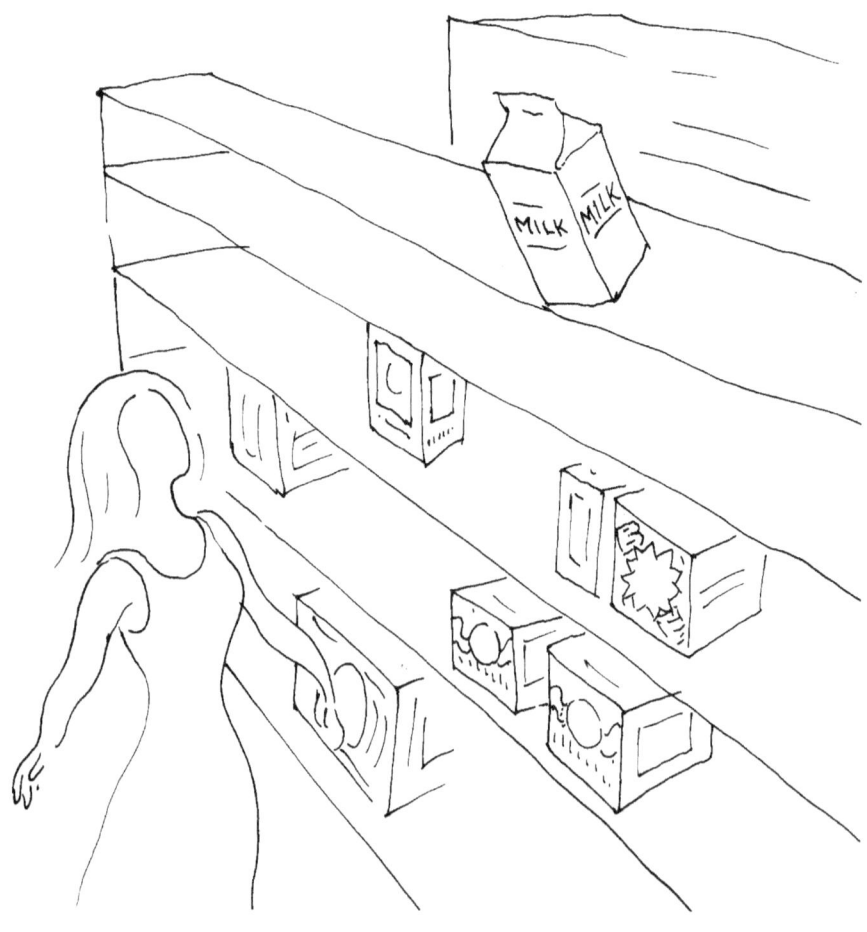

Because our grocery stores aren't large, I often have to go to more than one to find all of the items that I need. Although customer service was the bigger challenge in the new supermarket, an older competing market had a different issue. I had a problem with items placed on high shelves. When the stock was low, the remaining items were often pushed back so that I, as a short person, couldn't reach them, and even a taller person would have trouble. This was especially an issue with staples, such as milk.

I can't change my height, but I can change the store layout. So I pointed out the problem to the store manager. The manager thanked me perfunctorily, but on subsequent shopping trips, I saw that he made no effort to fix the problem. I went back to him a bit more testily and told him that if he couldn't address the problem, I would go through Corporate. He didn't like this, but promised to address the issue. Of course, after giving him a little time to fix it, nothing changed.

I kept my promise and called Corporate to rectify the problem. Immediately, things changed. *Remember to follow through on promises, otherwise nothing changes.* This particular manager avoids my gaze when he sees me, although other managers couldn't be more helpful. So I'm unpopular with one, but regarded cordially by others. But I managed to solve the problem. I can now reach most items, and the shelves with barren front space and full rear space are fixed. (Bottom line here is that I spend too much time in the supermarket, but that's a whole other issue.)

WOULD YOU LIKE YOUR TRASH PICKED UP OR DELIVERED?

I hate snow. It's white and pretty for about an hour after a snowfall, and then it turns gray and becomes a nuisance when you have to get out and get things done. I never could understand people who love snow. Give me heat any day—at least you don't have to shovel it.

During the week between Christmas and New Year's Day, we had a snowstorm. My street was due for recycling pickup three days after the storm. The roads were cleared, the sun was shining, and people were out and about. No pickup. Why did they forget us?

I called the Refuse Department. The person manning the phones said that he'd try to reach the trucks. He told me that if we didn't have pickup by 3 PM that day to call back at 8 AM the next day to make sure that they would come back to my street. Of course, there was no pickup that day, so I called at 8 AM the next day.

A different man answered and said that he couldn't guarantee pickup, that the snow had caused the problem, and it was a holiday week. In more than 25 years of living in this area, they've always been efficient, and I never had a weather related trash problem before that. So, why was I having one now?

"My trashcans overfloweth, and my neighbors and I really need pickup. It's early in the morning and the snow is cleared!" I said. Of course, I asked to speak with his manager. Of course, he was the only one there, or so he said.

What do you do during a holiday week when you are dealing with the government and someone telling you that he is the only game in town? You find a way to go around him.

He was in the Refuse Department. Who is in charge of the Refuse Department? Someone in the township, of course. I was about to call the general township number when I spotted Public Works. I called that number and asked to speak with a manager. As it turned out, I was speaking with a Public Works supervisor. When I explained the story, he responded that this snow job (literally) was ridiculous. My neighbors and I had our recycling picked up within a couple of hours.

Government can be a challenge. Years ago, when we lived in the city, our trash pickup suddenly stopped three weeks after a snowstorm. When I called the City Refuse Department and explained the problem, the person on the phone said that it had snowed. I responded that the snow was three weeks ago.

"Well, we're behind," she said.

"Yeah—but behind what?" I thought.

Better yet, many years ago, there was a city strike, although a few offices were still open for some reason. I went to pay my water bill in person, and I was the only customer there. There was a queue rope. But with no one there, pushing a baby stroller, check in hand, I just went to the front of the rope.

"You need to go through the line," the person behind the counter said.

"There's no one here, so why would I need to go through the line?" I asked.

"Because I might not see you," she responded. How do you argue that one? I couldn't help laughing. She didn't get it. That's okay; I got the water bill paid anyway.

CELLING YOUR SOUL

THE CELL PHONE GAME

IN THE OLD DAYS...

Once upon a time, long ago, we lived in a world without cell phones. People had landlines. You paid for your phone, which was not expensive. The options were minimal—just design differences and long distance calls. You paid a monthly phone bill, usually about $15 to $30. Simple. Now, cell phones are far more complicated, and I don't know anyone who hasn't had a problem with his or her cell phone carrier. (The same applies to cable companies. More about that later.)

IN THE NEW WORLD...

There is a question that I've never been able to resolve. Land line and cell phone bills often vary by a small amount each month—from a few cents to a little over a dollar. I can understand monthly variation in water or electric bills because usage varies. But when there are no extra phone services in a given month, why the variation in charges? Not much money/ not an issue worth chasing. Or is it?

I've asked several vendor contacts the reason for this fluctuation. I received a range of answers—none of which made sense to me. This reminds me of the movie *Office Space*. In the film, a group of employees in a miserable corporation develop a plot to shave a percentage of a cent off of each transaction, believing that the amount wouldn't be missed and they'd make enough money to leave. (The corporation was so miserable that they even confiscated mumbling Milton's precious red stapler. I saw a red stapler in a store and wanted to send it to Milton. I realized that I didn't have Milton's address. Then I remembered that Milton wasn't real.) The embezzlers made a fortune. Do the vendors in my life and your life make an illegitimate fortune on these small variations in charges? I can't answer that one, but it's something to think about.

The choice of phone model, features, and plan options with cell phones can be complicated. I had so many problems with my last cell phone company that I had a special manager assigned to my contract. A significant percentage of my bills were incorrect. Figuring out the bill almost required a Ph.D. in math.

My escalated contacts really did try to fix the problem. They arranged refunds for incorrect billing and negotiated courtesy credits for my time and inconvenience. Ultimately, however, after escalating past my special manager, going to Regional managers, up through Executive areas, and even with hundreds of dollars in Courtesy Credits, I had to change cell phone carriers. It just wasn't worth the angst with each bill. I finally made my way into the Legal department by networking with the management contacts that I found along the way. They let me out of my contract without charging the early termination fee. They probably had a party when I left. They could have at least offered me a piece of cake. But, here we had a Win/Win for all—I was rid of them and they were rid of me.

My family switched to another cell phone carrier. While both companies have their pros and cons, I'm generally happier now—except when I've experienced problems.

HARDWARE OR HARD WEAR?

Everyone in my family has had cell phone problems. Our problems and how I resolved them:

1) Tracy had a problem with her Blackberry. For no reason, it started to drop more calls than usual, and it was often difficult to hear her. Now I know how Alexander Graham Bell must have felt when he experimented with his first phone.

The cell phone company swapped out her phone under warranty. Within three months, she started to have the same problems. Because the newest smartphone would have been her next choice when her contract renewed three months later, it didn't seem unreasonable to ask for it now given the fact that she had become a muffled or nonexistent voice on the other end of the line—all over the course of two defective phones in a short period of time. The cell phone company wouldn't give her the newer smartphone, apparently based on policy issues with the carrier and the smartphone manufacturer. However, I had two creative solutions:

> A) Swap to the newer smartphone at the regular price, but do a courtesy adjustment to the monthly service bill so that the cost would balance out to $0. This would avoid any policy issues.

B) Give Tracy a phone with her current features and we'd do the upgrade in three months. The bottom line was that she needed a phone that worked with the same features that were on her previous phone.

Although I was dealing with an escalated area, the contact wasn't very good. She told me that she would give Tracy a basic phone without any new features and no other compensation until her contract rolled over. I responded that this was unacceptable. She responded with the automatic company call closure: "Thank you for choosing us." This didn't work for me. Keep it up and I won't be "choosing you" for much longer.

I went up the ladder again, to a higher level escalated contact by going through the Executive area again. I reached my current "go to" person, who understood our inconvenience and the excessive amount of time spent on this issue. She resolved the smartphone problem and also offered a credit that would equal the amount of my bill for that month. That was fair. Now, they kept a customer. Deal done!

2) As a technology-challenged person, I had a very basic phone, which died. After I replaced it, I found a One Time Upgrade charge of $18 on my next bill. I called Customer Service to ask what service was rendered for the Upgrade charge. I was told that this fee supported the store staff time to explain options and to work with the customer on use of the phone features. This didn't make sense to me. I countered with the fact that Howard and I had bought a new dishwasher. The salesman spent time going over choices and explaining how the dishwasher worked. We paid for the dishwasher. There was no charge to upgrade from our last dishwasher. As a longtime customer with a clear argument, it wasn't difficult to have the Upgrade fee rebated.

3) After making the change on Tracy's phone, I noticed a $30 Usage fee for her line, and $2.40 on my line on my next bill. I didn't access data from my flip phone, and Tracy had a Data

Usage plan. I learned that there had been billing errors when Tracy was going through her hardware difficulties. I was able to get a full credit for that month's bill. The credit took care of the Usage charges and was added compensation for my time and aggravation to resolve the problem.

Look at bills closely after any change to phone service. You will often see unanticipated and consumer unfriendly Corporate charges (like the one-time Upgrade fee) as well as errors on usual charges.

4) Tracy and Jonah were married shortly after buying the new phone. They wanted to be on a family plan together. (I was gaining a son-in-law and losing a phone bill—that worked for me!) However, the store told them that they couldn't go on a family plan unless one of them changed their number because they had two different area codes. Of course, neither of them wanted to make the change.

Because requiring a phone number change made no sense to me, I checked with my local store and got the same story. I went back to my escalated cell phone company contact. She was clear that the store staff was incorrect and arranged for Tracy and Jonah to go on their own family plan. As a courtesy, she credited them $200 towards their bill based on the misinformation that they had received and their time spent dealing with the problem. I also worked with her and with two managers above her in order to make sure that store staff would be educated about plan options because I was sure this was not a single store issue. If it happened to us, it would happen to someone else.

5) For some time, when Jonah called, I could hardly hear him and the calls often dropped. When we reconnected after a dropped call, I asked him if this was his new norm. He told me that he had been having problems, and had contacted the cell phone Customer Service line and gone into the stores. He had spoken with several people over the course of several months. Their response across the board, including supervisors, was

that he needed a piece of equipment in order to have adequate service. And, despite the fact that this was the phone company's problem, he would have to purchase the equipment. Not good!

Since the problem was on their equipment and service, it wasn't reasonable for Jonah to pay for the company driven problems. The amount of time he spent in dealing with the company plus the inconvenience and time lost on fuzzy and dropped calls was also unreasonable. His time was worth something, and the lack of problem solving skills on the phone company's side was unacceptable.

I told him that I would take care of it by getting in touch with my Executive contact. When I did, she assigned someone to reach out to him. Within a couple of hours, he heard from that contact, who explained that the stores couldn't give him the equipment without charging him, but she could rebate the cost on his next bill. Problem solved. Creative thinking translated to a great customer service experience.

6) When Cory got his new phone and I reviewed the next bill, once again I found an extra charge. Yes, that infamous One Time Upgrade fee. But I was a little confused when I saw an extra charge of $36. I was looking for the standard $18 charge.

I called Customer Service and reached a representative who confirmed that the charge was accurate. Although I wasn't deluding myself into thinking that my last cell phone adventure would eliminate Upgrade fees (but I had hoped), I wasn't anticipating that they would increase the fee!

When I asked for a credit, again using my rationale that I've been a longtime customer and posed the question about what service was rendered with the Upgrade charge, the representative said: "This is our policy." I repeated my expectation that he would credit the fee and that no other outcome was acceptable. Once again, he simply said: "This is our policy." It seems that I was talking to a robot. *Don't waste your time arguing with robots.* I asked for a supervisor. The supervisor was savvy enough to see my long relationship with the company, and saw a long chain of notes showing prior credit on this type of fee, as well as documentation of my long string of cell phone adventures. She immediately credited the fee.

I was really hoping that this would be my last cell phone adventure—at least for a while. Hope may have been out there, but reality trumped hope.

THE EXTRATERRESTRIAL PHONE ON LIFE SUPPORT

Howard had been sounding garbled when he called from his cell phone. Maybe he needed a new phone. We went into the phone store. The salesperson cheerfully told us that his problem was a common "end of life" issue. "End of life" issue—are we talking about ICUs or cell phones? The new reality is that our smartphones take on a life of their own. Anthropomorphized, they control us. I feel as if I'm writing science fiction.

Once again, beware of change on a wireless plan. As Howard made the purchase, the salesperson accessed his account information to make the transfer. She used a handheld gadget that pulled up his information magically. (I still feel like I'm writing science fiction. Who would have thought that Maxwell Smart and his shoe phone would turn into this!) She was trying to ensure that all options were in place. I noticed that there wasn't a charge showing unlimited data access. We thought that he had this service, but we hadn't memorized all of his plan details. To avoid problems later, we called the wireless Customer Service line from the store. Yes, Howard did have unlimited data. Customer Service was great—the representative talked to the salesperson in the store and together, they found a creative way to make the unlimited data plan reappear. The salesperson then explained that this option had been phased out, and only people who had it previously could be grandfathered back in.

I am so convinced that this was a cute Corporate trick. If the option doesn't show at the start of a new contract and you haven't memorized your features and billing information, confusion, or, more accurately, the wireless company, reigns.

Data charges are expensive, and without an appropriate plan that coordinates with the customer's needs, the customer is screwed. If you realize that your charges don't look right when you receive your next bill, or even after a couple of cycles, go right back to the company to fix it. It's just easier if you can catch it at the start. If Howard and I experienced this and were confused, what about everyone else? I think that we're not alone. (Still sounds like science fiction—the Controllers misleading the Pod people?) Meanwhile, how much does this company or any other carrier make on these misleading transactions?

I told the technician that buying a new phone is traumatic. He looked at me like I was nuts. Tech salespeople in the cell phone world have no sense of humor. Maybe they're not real; maybe they're just Pods.

SMALL BUSINESSES/ BIG PROBLEMS

Dealing with small business can be a challenge. You can't call an Executive office to find an escalated contact and there usually isn't clear oversight where there can be a penalty for problematic practices. However, there is often a way to turn a wrong into a right.

BEJEWELED AND BE SCREWED

I used to have a close relationship with Jerry, my jeweler. When I started buying pieces from him about 20 years ago, he was pretty honest and reasonable. I trusted him, and he knew it. I worked with him to design pieces that I couldn't find elsewhere, and I found that he was always careful to assure that the quality of workmanship and materials was up to my expectations. Although I wasn't his highest spending customer, I was a steady customer for many years.

At some point, however, something happened, and he violated my trust. Now he is my ex-jeweler.

I had an old ring that didn't fit well, and I wanted it redesigned. It was a very high-quality ring so I decided to use the same stones in a new design. The design was pretty simple and straightforward—nothing exotic and far less complicated than other items that Jerry had made for me. When it was finished, I found that there was a stone so sunken that it looked like it was missing. I gave it back to him to fix it. It came back only slightly improved. Before I could send it back again, another stone fell out. After sending it back four times, it still wasn't adequate, let alone good. Unlike other pieces I had purchased from him, it was a piece of junk—I needed to return it. Much to my surprise, Jerry refused to give me a refund or exchange the ring for a fair price. Instead, he wanted to give me scrap value at much less than what I had paid for the ring.

Here is a situation where trust had become a problem. Jerry owned his business. I had trusted him. Now I was stuck with a defective ring. What was my recourse? I argued for an exchange based on our history together. I also had a legitimate argument that the ring was poorly made and it wasn't what we had agreed upon in terms of quality, despite numerous repairs. It wasn't unreasonable to expect that our relationship and long history would work as negotiating points when I had a legitimate issue on a defective item. I was very wrong on that expectation. Something had changed. Was Jerry just being greedy? Was business off? Was I not important enough since I wasn't spending a fortune? It doesn't matter—he was taking advantage of me. And that isn't acceptable.

My first recoupment strategy was to point out the flaws in the ring, and that I was one of his first customers, had been a customer for many years, and hoped that I could remain a customer. I also told Jerry that I was certain that he had made money on this item, and if there was some cost to him to make the exchange, because it was his problem and not mine, he

SMALL BUSINESSES/BIG PROBLEMS

should eat the cost. I also told him that if I couldn't trust him, he would lose a customer. There was nowhere else to go since I was dealing with the owner. My final statement was to be clear that Jerry had just lost a customer, as well as any future customers that I might have sent to him. Sometimes, you just do what you can, until there is nothing else to do. (I thought about walking down the street wearing a sandwich board sign, advertising his sleaze. Tempting as that was, it just wasn't me.)

Having stopped at what I thought was the point of no return, both figuratively and literally, I was resigned to living with a crappy ring that I wouldn't wear often, if at all. I thought about scrapping it with another jeweler, so I went to see Sam. I had known Sam for a long time and trusted him to give me an expert and objective opinion. As an expert on repairs, I thought that he might be able to do something to make a wearable ring out of this piece of junk. To my surprise, he said that many of the stones were poor quality, and the setting was so poor that it wasn't worth re-doing. I had known that the ring was set poorly, but was surprised at the stone issue, since I had confirmation that the stones were good ones before I gave them to Jerry for the new design. I thought that Jerry and I had reached bottom before I got to Sam. I was wrong. One more problem in this train wreck.

What could I do about the situation? Jerry was still the owner and was clear in his unwillingness to back his product. Here I was, about six months downstream and with no real options. Realizing that Jerry probably wouldn't do much and that I had nothing to lose, I decided to make him realize that I wasn't stupid and that he was a sleaze. Sometimes, when there's nothing left, having the last word can provide some satisfaction. Janis Joplin was so right when she sang: "Freedom's just another word for nothing left to lose."

How could I communicate my fury without coming across like a crazoid? (Crazoid doesn't buy much in terms of action on the other end.) What was Jerry's vulnerable spot? I knew that I could figure it out. *The key is to remain totally calm and immovable, and to make statements that couldn't be challenged.* I called Jerry. He greeted me like an old friend.

"Hi, Mauree! How are you?"

"Fine, Jerry, and how are you?" I replied, before moving in for the kill. "Jerry, you remember the ring problem. I know that you aren't going to do anything, but I just needed you to know that I took it to someone I know and trust to see if I could salvage it, and he told me that the setting was really poor and too many of the stones were no good. I pretty much knew the problem, but I have to tell you that to hear this from another jeweler, and to find that the value is less than 25% of the cost is pretty shocking. So, we've already had the discussion about the fact that you're unwilling to do anything, but I just had to let you know what I found. I'm not going to argue about having given you good stones and getting poor quality stones in return. I don't know if this is you or your setter, but either way… And I know that there is nothing that you are willing to do to address it. But just so you know, I am aware of how bad the ring really is, even though I started out by giving you a very good quality ring to work with."

I knew that I would hit a nerve. And I did. And, I aborted his ability to argue by emphasizing that I knew his position and at that point, wasn't asking for anything (or so it seemed). I wasn't in an accusing mode—I was simply stating facts. After this, I moved on to my most pointed strategy.

"Jerry, I know that you won't do anything to make this right. And, I'm not asking for anything," I began. *I challenged him with a clear but softly stated observation that he couldn't argue.* "But I won't embarrass myself by selling it for low scrap value, and I also will not keep this ring in my home. I'll stop by at some point and return the ring to you. I'll be back." (How

Schwarzenegger can you get? Howard nicknamed me "The Maurinator").

"Mauree, I won't take the ring back," Jerry responded.

"I know that," I replied. "I'm not bothering to ask for anything, since I know that you won't back your product. I just don't want it, so you can do whatever you want with it."

Jerry: "I won't take it back,"

Mauree: "Well, of course you will. I'll walk in and lay it on your counter. You can throw it in the trash, flush it down the toilet, frame it as an example of how you pulled one over on me, or walk after me and throw it in the street. I don't care what you do with it, but it's not staying in this house."

Jerry: "I'll mail it back to you."

Mauree: "That's fine, and I'll bring it back to you, and we can go back and forth for the rest of our lives. I need to go now, but I'm glad that we had this little talk, so I'll see you next time I'm in New York."

I could feel the agitation on his end. *Most importantly, though, I found a strategy to let him know that this will never go away.* Jerry certainly realized that I wasn't bluffing. Although I knew that I had penetrated his armor and was hoping that I could accomplish something, I wasn't sure that he would do anything. While my goal was to have him make it right, I didn't bank on that, based on our more recent history. I simply had to try. If I couldn't accomplish something concrete, at least I was clear with him that I was totally aware that he tried to put one over on me—I'm not stupid.

It took less than ten minutes for Jerry to call me back and say: "We do have a history together, and even if this is the last piece that I ever make for you, I want to get it right. I'll email you tomorrow with a plan." The next day, I received an email saying that he would make it right, even if he had to make a new ring from scratch. And that's just what he did.

The point here is that I found his vulnerable spot; I challenged his business ethics. And most importantly, my tone and my language made it clear that I wasn't just making threats to keep bringing the ring back to him—I would really do it. Jerry heard me, chose to avoid a lifetime of ring exchange, and was pushed to make it right. Now I have a ring that's not my favorite—it's a little tainted by the experience—but it is a decent piece, better made, with quality stones, and wearable.

SOMETHING'S FISHY

I have trained my husband to like fish. We have a dinnertime routine. He calls me on the way home from work and asks what's for dinner. I tell him that we're having fish. "I have a long day at work, and I'm coming home to fish?" he always complains. I tell him which fish and how I'm preparing it, reminding him that he liked it the last time. He is skeptical. When he finally takes a bite, he admits that it's good. Same routine every time. Howard is not demented. It's simply that old memories can sometimes obscure recent experience until current events take over. I attribute his final surrender to my finding new recipes and a really good local fish store.

I have been going to the same fish store for years now. I usually need three-quarters of a pound of fish. The staff are pleasant and I generally get what I want, or close to it. Until the day that I didn't.

There is a woman at the fish store who is sometimes pleasant and sometimes not, but not usually a problem. When I asked for three-quarters of a pound of trout, she told me that they were all about half a pound. A half pound was too little, and a full pound was too much. No one else was waiting, so that asking her to go through the pieces wasn't an unreasonable request. She went through a few and then told me that she "knows the fish" and that none were the right size. She wouldn't look further or cut a piece.

"Why don't you get something else?" she said. Howard expected trout that night, I wanted trout, and hadn't had a problem with trout in the past. Reluctantly, I settled for a pound.

As I started to walk away, I thought, "Why shouldn't I be able to have the amount that I need?" I went back and asked for the manager. Next came one of my favorite lines: "I *AM* the manager."

"I want to talk to the owner," I replied.

"She isn't here," Fish Lady responded. I was stonewalled—or was I?

After I got home, I called the fish store, and asked for the manager. Lucky me—I reached Fish Lady again. One more time, I heard, "She isn't here." I asked for a number to reach her.

"I don't give out her number." Fed up, I asked Fish Lady to leave my number so that the owner could call me back.

What would you expect in this situation? Not much. Of course, I didn't receive a call back. What do you do when you are dealing with a small local business and can't get to the top for resolution? You can't call a Corporate office. You've reached the manager—maybe. The owner wasn't on site. *Think creatively!*

How did I think creatively to resolve this customer service problem?

1. *Who would have oversight over this business?* The store is located in a Farmers market. The Farmers market is located in a shopping center. I Googled the name of the shopping center and found the management office.

2. *I called the shopping center's management office* and spoke with the general manager.

3. *I stated my problem clearly.* I was receiving poor customer service and couldn't get to the owner so that I could report it. Politely, but clearly, I told him that I can shop anywhere—there are other resources in the area. He agreed that I received poor service, and he did want my business in his Farmers market. If enough people have this type of experience, they won't shop there. This can destroy a business, especially if no one says anything so that the situation can be rectified. I also noticed that there had been several businesses that left the market, so maintaining this tenant was important to the shopping center management. He got me where I needed to be by telling me that the owner has two stores and is

only at this store on weekends. He gave me her name and a number to reach her at her other store.

4. *I called the store owner* and told her my sad fish tale. Of course, Fish Lady had never given her my message. The owner didn't want me to find another fish market, and said that she would address the problem, which she did immediately.

The next time that I bought fish, Fish Lady couldn't have been nicer. Even better, there was a new face—the owner's sister, who introduced herself, and made sure that I walked out with exactly what I needed.

What did I accomplish? I made the owner aware of a problem that she didn't know about previously. She addressed the problem, evidenced by the fact that the formerly not so helpful Fish Lady was waiting for me with open arms, and there was additional management on site in the form of the owner's sister. I win because I continue to shop there, and can shop effortlessly now by buying what I need without an argument and without paying for more than I want to buy. Fish Lady has become consistently friendly and I also now have a dedicated staffer who always gets me what I need. The owner also wins because she keeps a customer's business and doesn't have the bad word of mouth that can occur when a customer is unhappy. Like I said before, Win/Win is always good.

Be creative to get to the top and don't give up until you get there

GRILL OF MY DREAMS

Barbecuing in nice weather is one of life's small pleasures. With sunshine and warmth, the smell of grilling makes a lovely day perfect. A couple of years ago, it was time to replace our old gas grill. It started, but we usually had to start it with a match. The last few times, even the matches broke. It looked like we'd have to replace the matches, too.

Comparison shopping is always a good idea, especially for a significant purchase. Where to look? We tried three options—our local independently owned hardware store, a big box store, and the local family-owned appliance store. We found that the price for the grill at the big box store was a little lower than the hardware store's price. However, the big box store charges for delivery, evening out the pricing. We would prefer to have used the hardware store, because dealing with them is easy—no five hour windows for delivery, as well as local access if there is a problem. The only problem with the hardware store was that they wouldn't take the old grill, creating a nuisance for us because we would have to find someone to take it away.

We hadn't originally thought about going to the appliance store, thinking that they only sold appliances—logical thought. But, you never know, and *it's always a good idea to think broadly.* Since this store had been dependable and had taken away old appliances in the past, we checked their website and saw that they did sell grills. We always had good experiences with them in the past, and a friend had also been pleased when I referred her to them for a new washer, so this seemed like a very good option. However, we had a few communication problems with them earlier in the year when we needed a repair and had difficulty getting a call back when we left a message for their repair service. This time, we decided to send an email to check out cost, delivery options, and whether they would take the old grill. One email—no response; second email—no response. This just wasn't like them, but we now had a few instances where no response occurred. What to do? *Pick up the phone when email doesn't work.*

I went right to the owner because he had a reputation to maintain. I thought that he would want to know about the problem and would probably be responsible about fixing it. When he picked up, I told him about the recent history of lack of response, focusing on the emails. We both learned something here. I learned that they were still responsive. The owner learned that the marketing service for the website was problematic for email. He didn't even know where the emails were going and hadn't seen them.

When he explained that he didn't know how the email worked, I suggested that he take off the email address, since lack of response wasn't in sync with the good service that they normally offer. He also needed to talk to the marketing company. They should have been promoting him, not morphing him into the Invisible Man. If I hadn't followed through and told him about the problem, he wouldn't have known, and would have lost my business and probably other business as well. *Silence never yields results.*

I found that this store wouldn't charge for delivery and would take the old grill. We purchased our grill without hassle. For my inconvenience in having to chase him down, the owner even threw in a grill cover without charge—I didn't have to ask.

Grill delivered—we barbecued chicken that night.

BURIED ALIVE

There are times when a locally owned business won't make an adjustment and you just have to make your point and walk away, looking for some other type of resolution. As in the burial plot caper.

While most women receive a diamond ring when they become engaged, I didn't. Howard and I had just finished school and had been working for all of a few weeks when we got engaged. Being practical and penniless, we decided that it was more important to save for furniture than to put a diamond on my finger.

Although I didn't get a diamond, I did receive a more unusual engagement present from my future in-laws. They cheerfully informed me that now that Howard and I were engaged, I would be the lucky owner of a cemetery plot, since they had purchased a group for the family. I interpreted this as a "Welcome to the family" comment—not a "We will bury you" comment.

Many years later, my in-laws died, and the plots were left to Howard. We weren't so sure that we wanted to be buried in the boondocks where the cemetery was located, and thought that we might want to sell the plots. When I had to deal with the cemetery director, I found out just how predatory this industry can be.

I called to inquire about the cost of plots. Our plots were in an older area of the cemetery, and the director said that they would sell for about $2500 each. He offered me the $990 that my in-laws had paid for the group of eight plots about 45 years earlier. That was a shocker. The director explained that there are newer sections of the cemetery, but that there is some demand for older plots, since there are families who want to be close to loved ones even after they're dead, and there are very few plots available in the older section of the cemetery. He was telling me that there was a market for our plots, although a small one, minimizing it in order to lowball me.

    I explained that I certainly wouldn't expect retail value of $2500 and understand the cost of doing business with a middle man, but the discrepancy between the $123.75 originally paid for each plot versus the $2500 selling price was a bit much. His point was that there are maintenance costs for running a cemetery. I pointed out that for all of these years with our plots—and, whether we kept them or sold them—he was probably only mowing the lawn. I'm not sure how his broader business costs impacted on our situation. Since there was some demand, there would probably be a sale eventually. Even if he paid us 50% of his pricing, he would still be making money. If we kept the plots or sold them on our own, his profit would be $0. My argument had no impact. He held the cards and didn't have the sense or integrity to respond with a reasonable offer.

    I asked to speak with the owner. He said that the owner would tell me the same thing. *I can speak for myself; I don't go through middlemen.* I told Mr. Director that I would speak to the owner, who just happened to be the owner of a local funeral home. This was a real boon for Mr. Owner—get them in the chapel and nail them in the ground. In a last ditch (no pun intended) attempt to rope us into his agenda, Mr. Director did tell me that we could pre-pay burial costs to avoid inflation. The discussion about selling plots turned into "How can we make death even more profitable?" But it is what it is. I did some research and found that it is pretty much the industry standard to offer original price on buy back. But the argument on our side is that we were probably in the minority, with plots that were sold so many years ago that the discrepancy in price was much greater than today's norm.

I did speak with Mr. Owner. He was obnoxious, and this proved to be the rare instance where the owner did stand the same ground as Mr. Director. (pun intended this time)

So, if you're looking for a career where you've got your population by the tail (or some other eventually dead body part), by all means, think of the death industry. With no leverage, I finished by telling them that we would keep the plots, sell them on our own, or wait until his industry grew a conscience and integrity. (Although we'd probably be dead by then.) Or, maybe we'd like to see the plots and just might bring a picnic lunch to at least get our money's worth. In the end, Howard and I agreed that the picnic would be a bit over the top, not wanting to disrespect the dead and their living relatives.

I couldn't accomplish what I set out to do, but I made the effort and I made my point. I'll just keep this issue buried in the back of my mind (yes, another pun), and if the right time arises, who knows, maybe I'll have another opportunity to take a shot at selling the plots sometime in the future.

TRUE STORIES I COULDN'T POSSIBLY MAKE UP

NEVER CLEAN YOUR SUNGLASSES WITH NAIL POLISH REMOVER— A MANAGER HORROR STORY

I am a sunglass addict. I can't walk outside without them, and they are an easy way to vary my accessory routine. I am always careful with them—I never throw them into my purse without a case, never push them on top of my head, use a soft cloth to clean them. I just wear them and treat them gently.

One sunny day, I went to put on my favorite pair. I found that the bridge (the part that goes over your nose) was all weird—the plastic was rough, as if someone had used sandpaper on them. I have never used sandpaper on my sunglasses. Why were they dying on me?

What to do? This shouldn't happen; there had to be a manufacturing flaw that caused some type of deterioration. I trotted off to the store to have them replaced. (These were not inexpensive; for this level of purchase, I make it a habit to keep a copy of the receipt. That way, there is no question about where they were purchased—although in some stores, if you have the credit card that you used to purchase the item, the store can look in their system to verify the purchase.)

The salesperson quickly saw that the frame was defective and was willing to exchange them for a new pair, but needed a manager's approval. She called Kathy, the manager on call. Or, the manager from hell. Kathy took a look at the sunglasses, saw that they were damaged, and told me that it must have been my fault. I explained that it wasn't my fault—I did nothing but wear them and take good care of them, and their death wasn't on my conscience. Rather, their death should be the manufacturer's problem, and by extension, the store's problem as the middleman. I bought them from the store, not from the manufacturer. Kathy looked me straight in the eye when she said:

"You used nail polish remover on them." Nail polish remover?

"Why would anyone use nail polish remover on sunglasses? And if I had, wouldn't the whole frame be damaged?" I responded.

She smiled sweetly—saccharine sweetly—and said: "I'm sorry, but I can't take them back; you used nail polish remover on them".

My response: "We're done here; I need to speak with your manager—NOW!" She replied that she was the only manager in the store at the time.

When a first line manager tells you this, especially one who sounds like she lives on Mars, you know that she's not the last word; she's lying. You need to stand firm and go around her. How did I do that? First, I told her that I didn't believe that she was the only manager in the store, and that I wanted the Store Manager, rather than her, the Department/On Call manager. She continued to stand there with her patronizing smile and told me that the Store Manager was out, and she was the only manager in the store.

Kathy wouldn't budge. Of course, neither would I. Aside from the fact that she was very strange, *there is rarely, if ever, only one manager in a department store.* I glared and told her that I would locate another manager. And I did. How did I do it? I walked over to the next department and explained that I had been insulted by Kathy and needed to speak to another store manager, preferably a higher-level manager. The salesperson immediately located Kathy's manager.

Kathy was the only manager in the store? I didn't think so and now I knew that this wasn't the case! Kathy's manager exchanged the sunglasses for me, and although she did what I asked her to do, she seemed to do it grudgingly. Having experienced such awful customer service that day, I decided to call the Store Manager's office later. When I reached her voicemail, I left a message saying that I had been insulted by a lunatic manager and needed her to know about the situation. (If I didn't get a call back, I would locate the Regional Manager for the store chain and let that person deal with the situation. *I could locate that person by going through the store's main location or through Corporate Headquarters.)*

I received a call back very quickly. Not only was the Store Manager horrified to hear what happened, she told me that she had actually been in the store at the time that the problem occurred. As compensation for the problem, aside from addressing it with Kathy, she sent me $50 in store discounts. I wasn't looking for the discounts in this situation, but it wasn't inappropriate, given how horribly Kathy had handled the situation.

When someone on the first line tells you that they are the highest authority but they are giving you a hard time and bad information, you can assume that they aren't at the top of the chain. In fact, I've pretty much found that they are never at the top of the chain.

Years ago, I was dealing with an insurance agent who worked in the family business. He wasn't doing what I needed him to do. (Sons and daughters falling into a family business can be great but sometimes not so great. You may get a family member who takes pride in the business and really understands customer service. Sometimes you get a family member who defaults into the business and thinks that he's the king. In this case, I was dealing with the self-proclaimed king.) After a few moments with him, going nowhere, I said:

"I need to speak with the president of the company."

"I'm the president of the company," he replied.

"No you're not. Your father is." He had no response to that.

When I reached his father, he started to laugh.

"What did you say to him? He was actually sputtering when he told me about this!" the president said. Dad resolved the issue.

As Mel Brooks said, "It's good to be the king."

I'M NOT A BANK ROBBER— HOW I ALMOST GOT ARRESTED WHEN I TRIED TO DEPOSIT MONEY IN THE BANK

Generally, when you think of a police raid on a bank, someone is trying to rob the bank. Not in my little banking adventure—the bank nearly called the police when I tried to put money *into* the bank!

When Cory was a college student, it seemed that he always needed money. (What college student doesn't?) He banked with a large national bank. We bank with a different large local bank. Howard and I have a joint account. Howard was on Cory's account in case of emergencies. I was not. When Cory needed money, Howard would write a check and I would go to the local branch of Cory's bank to deposit it. Howard usually made the check out to himself, but for some reason, this time he made the check out to me and wrote "For Deposit Only," with Cory's name and bank account number on the back. I would endorse it when I got to the bank teller and deposit it. Simple? Not this time.

I went up to the teller, and handed her the deposit. With her reaction, you would have thought that I had handed her a note: "Give me all of your cash." But I didn't do that—this was just a deposit slip and a check. She asked me if I was on Cory's account.

"No, but why is that an issue, since I'm depositing a check?" I inquired.

"We can't accept this deposit," she replied. Huh? Her explanation was that this was their policy. After a few "I don't understand" comments from me, I finally got her to explain that she couldn't accept the check because I wasn't on Cory's account and that it could be a bad check. I pointed out that even if I were on the account, I still could write a bad check. Also, the "Six Degrees of Kevin Bacon" game applies here—I was on my account with Howard, and Howard was on the account with Cory, so the money was coming from the same account. Remember, I was depositing money, not withdrawing it. I asked for the manager. The manager stonewalled me—this was their policy, no exceptions. Bad answer.

How do you get beyond a situation like this? You're stonewalled by the teller and the manager, and there's nowhere else to go within this small branch of the bank. Do you do nothing? Do you leave? Of course not. I asked for the number of the Regional Manager, and right there in the bank, I called her on my cell phone. She listened to my problem and asked to speak with the bank manager. After 45 minutes, and calls to who knows who, someone at a higher level finally approved the deposit.

How did I get my goal accomplished? I immediately saw that no one in the bank had a clue about customer service, nor was anyone able to think outside of the box. If I were in a management position, I would look for logical ways to solve the problem. The manager could have placed a call to a higher authority immediately, rather than having me do it. Also, I had deposited through this teller before, so I was a known face.

With no ally within the bank, I was on my own—and clear that I was going to accomplish my goal. *My demeanor—standing straight, George glare, Belle tone, asking for the escalated contact (the Regional Manager)—and the fact that I didn't move—were all important in pushing the non-responsive bank manager to do what needed to be done.*

I told the manager I wasn't going anywhere without having that deposit placed in Cory's account. Since I had her in an unyielding position, she tried to intimidate me. That's when she said that she would call the police. This was a last ditch effort to divert and scare me. Obviously, it didn't work. I laughed—not the response she anticipated—and asked her what she would tell them when she called: "I have a woman here trying to make a deposit. Come quickly before she hands us the check!" The additional frustration that I created for her added incentive to make things work so that she could get me out of there. Yes, at that point, getting rid of me was her most important goal.

When I spoke with the Regional Manager later, she explained that the reason for the policy is that because I am not on Cory's account, I may have a hidden agenda with the intent to pass a bad check. The consequence would be that Cory would incur a $35 bad check fee on his account. The bank would have accepted the check if Howard had made it out to himself.

I later called the Executive Relations Department of the bank to see if I could get a better understanding of why the situation unfolded as it did. I reached a much more customer service friendly person who explained the policy and general banking regulations to me. Technically, the bank was right to reject the deposit, based on the fact that the policy was put in place because of Federal banking rules. But at least this representative understood my position. She understood that the bank manager could have offered better customer service to work with me and the people above her to resolve the issue without the extended stonewall that left me with a bad taste for this bank. She told me that there was a way to make an exception under some circumstances, and this was one of those circumstances.

I could live with the Federal regulations. (Actually, I can't—I think that they're bureaucratic and still don't see how this is a substantive protection for consumers. Better that they deal effectively with the bigger problems in the banking industry.) But I can't live with the awful customer service.

End of story—we've switched to online transfers.

MORE MANAGER TRICKS

DRESSING UP

Shopping with Tracy is one of life's special gifts. It's a gift for both of us, because we love to do it. It's often more of a gift for her because I end up paying the bill. ("A rose is a rose is a rose"—Gertrude Stein. "A mom is a mom is a mom"—Mauree Miller.)

We found a great summer dress that would work for so many occasions. I had planned well, taking her shopping when there was a special promotion throughout the store. This dress was now hers for a reasonable price. Without the promotion, it either would never go on sale or would be on sale at the end of the season, with only leftovers in the wrong size. Promotion time became the perfect shopping time.

The dress needed a simple alteration. Because she lives outside of the area, Tracy had to do that at her local branch. She needed proof of purchase in order to have the alteration done in the branch store. So we left the tags on the dress to document the purchase. The alteration process should have been easy, but it didn't turn out that way.

Problem One: When Tracy brought the dress to the store for fitting, the staff told her that she needed the receipt. Wrong! The computer-generated sticker on the back of the tag has all of the receipt information necessary for proof of purchase.

Problem Two: In order to address the lack of a receipt, the staff said that they had to go to the Administrative office to track down the purchase details. Wrong again! Here too, the tag sticker was sufficient.

Problem Three: As Tracy was having the dress pinned, she was told that the alteration cost was $65. This was waaaay overpriced. This should have been a $20–$30 alteration. (Mom, speaking from the voice of experience.)

Problem Four: While the seamstress pinned the dress, the staffer who had gone to find the receipt came back and said that she couldn't locate the receipt information and they couldn't do the alteration. Wrong information; bad service! And this was taking much too long. Tracy had spent an hour on this little project.

What do you do when you experience bad service, inconvenience and incorrect information? My daughter knew from long experience with her mother—*Get a manager!*

Which led to:

Problem Five: Tracy explained that the problem with the receipt made no sense, especially with the tag intact. And the charge seemed much too high, not to mention the excessive time to deal with this. Her request? Just do the alteration and reduce the charge based on the problematic experience. Although Tracy was on terra firma, the manager's response was that there was nothing that she could do. This was an unacceptable response. Tracy took off the dress and went to a tailor, who charged $25 for the alteration. (You see, I do know my alteration prices—right in my estimate range.)

What did Tracy do wrong? She didn't go above this manager. *When you reach a manager, and he/she doesn't make sense or satisfy your needs, go higher. You should also wonder if he/she really is the manager.*

Now, we get to the "Mommy manipulation". This is a little dynamic that Tracy and I have gone through many times, ever since she was little. She is annoyed about what happened. She knows that it should and can be fixed, but she isn't in take the time to do it mode. So she tells me. And she has me nailed—she knows that I can't just let it go and walk away. What do I do? As always, I fix it. (I have to work on that—she needs to do it herself. I'm getting worn out.)

I called the store. I didn't ask for the Department Manager; I went straight upwards. I asked for the Store Manager. I started by calling the main number for the store. I reached a National call center. When I called, the operator couldn't identify the manager in the branch store and couldn't connect me anywhere meaningful. This made no sense. *What do you do when you reach an unhelpful operator? Take his/her name and then call back. You will usually locate someone who does know what to do, and you should also report the last know-nothing.* On call back, I reached an operator who directed me to the Senior Manager on Duty, Alana.

Alana was great. She volunteered the name of the Store Manager and gave me his number for future reference. Alana confirmed my belief that the tag issue should not have been a problem. She also revealed, as I suspected, that the manager at the time of the problem was only an Assistant Manager. In a discreet manner, she essentially told me that the Assistant Manager didn't know what she was doing. My goal—get it fixed. Alana agreed to do just that. How would she fix it?

1. She promised to reach out to Tracy to get accurate details about the incident.

2. I asked her to arrange the alteration without charge (before I knew that Tracy had already gone elsewhere). She agreed to this.

3. She took the initiative to talk to the Associate Manager to educate her so that this wouldn't happen to anyone else.

4. She gave me her contact information in case I had problems in the future.

In other words, she got it right!

If the manager isn't getting it right, you're in the wrong place. Take the time to look for the right resource and the right resolution—it's worth it!

THE PHANTOM NIGHT MANAGER

There are corporations that are responsible and responsive. We've had several experiences with a particular hotel chain where the managers were really concerned about making sure that issues were addressed and that the guest is satisfied. Remember, it is in their best interest to make sure that guest services go smoothly—there are many hotel options out there and a dissatisfied guest is a guest who probably won't return. Not only is the guest important, word of mouth is important. Recommendations or bad reviews can be powerful for the reputation of a hotel, especially in this era when anyone can write an online review. This applies to many industries, but hotels are among the ultimate in the Service industry.

We had a problematic experience with a stay at this chain when our room was located above the pool area. Trying to take a nap, we found the noise overwhelming. When we tried to address the problem, we were directed to another room that was a quieter but less comfortable space. After the disrupted nap and the not so satisfactory move, I spoke with the manager. Based on the problems, along with several unsatisfactory interactions with front desk staff, the manager gave us a certificate for a complimentary one night stay. The certificate stated "Anytime." There was also a disclaimer stating that the certificate wasn't valid for a holiday weekend. Concluding that the handwritten "Anytime" trumped the disclaimer for holiday weekends, I made a reservation for a holiday weekend. The Reservations Manager tried to stonewall me based on the disclaimer, ignoring the handwritten override. It was only when I asked for a Hotel Manager that she agreed to make the reservation. The hotel wasn't busy—why would they alienate a guest in a situation like this?

After our stay, we had a $0 balance but then we found a $25 charge when we went online to check our credit card account. I called the hotel that evening and reached a front desk person. She curtly told me that this was probably a "hold" by the credit card company in the event of any incidentals. Since I hadn't experienced this previously (although I later found that this was correct) and the representative sounded like she couldn't care less, I told her that I would speak with a manager. Her response: "Whatever". (Yeah, honey—wait and I'll take care of "whatever".) In this quick interchange, I hadn't caught her name. I called back and reached Miranda. I said that I had just spoken with someone at the front desk and asked if she was that person. She told me that the person I'd spoken with had stepped away from the desk and I must have spoken with Belinda. At that point, with night staff and a non-urgent issue, I decided to call a manager the next day.

The Manager of Guest Services was genuinely concerned about the inappropriate response from his representative. The problem was that there was no Belinda working the desk. I had made a note of the date and time of the call. Based on this information, the manager's conclusion was that Miranda must have recognized my voice and thought that she would try to dupe me. Obviously, that didn't work. You can run—or lie—but you can't hide.

The manager took care of educating this disingenuous night staff person, and added Reward points to my account for my time in bringing the problem to his attention so that he could correct it. This manager definitely maintained my relationship, since he was clear that the behavior of the representative was unacceptable, he made himself readily available to hotel guests, and he was so obviously concerned about customer service.

The bottom line here is that you need to get to the right person in any setting in order to get the right answer. Many corporations have a call center that handles Executive inquiries. Some of these are helpful and others aren't. The Administrative Assistant to a CEO or president can often be a good resource—either to resolve the problem for you or to get you to the person who can do that. Sometimes it is better to go to an Executive contact in a specific area, such as a call to the VP of Operations. Basically, you need to go upward in the company, express your issue clearly, and ask to be pointed in the right direction. *You will know pretty quickly whether you were pointed to the right place. If you are hearing someone act responsively, if they hear your issue rather than parrot company policy, if they return your calls, if they give you options that make sense, then you are in the right place.*

I didn't have to go very far up with this hotel chain, but I found better service by going upward than the service I received from the Reservations Manager and the Night Manager who went into hiding.

I DON'T KNOW WHY ANYONE WOULD WANT TO SKIN A CAT BUT THERE'S MORE THAN ONE WAY TO DO IT

BUTTON UP AND MAKE IT SNAPPY

Winter is my least favorite season. I hate being cold and I dread snow and ice. In the winter, I drive the dirtiest car in my neighborhood, fearing that if I have my car washed, it will snow. My friend also has her superstitions about keeping the snow away. Her idea was better than mine. She had her eye on a coat, and had trouble justifying the purchase, since she has more coats than she could wear. Her brainstorm—if she bought this one, it could keep the snow away! This was an expensive way of making magic, but she did it anyway. Since it had been a mild winter on the East Coast the year that she bought the coat, she hadn't worn the coat at all that season—and was quick to take credit for the good weather. My car, her coat—between the two of us, we did okay weatherwise.

There is one problem in her coat story. She had mulled over the purchase for so long that by the time she bought the coat, the manufacturer's tag, with extra snaps attached, had somehow disappeared. This was the only coat left in her size so she grabbed it. But she really wanted the manufacturer's tag. More important, she needed the extra snaps.

As my friend searched for her tag and snaps, Howard lost a button from a coat he had bought a year ago that was made by the same manufacturer. I frantically searched through my button jar. (Yes, I have a button jar—full of extra buttons that come with new clothes and fun finds to make old clothes look unique. It's a fond holdover from my childhood, when I would play with the pile of buttons in my aunt's button jar while she cooked and chatted with my mother. I highly recommend button jars.) My downfall here was that my button jar wasn't organized, and I couldn't find the extra button for his coat. I'll work on my organizational skills some other time. But back to the problem at hand. How did we locate a replacement button?

Howard had a good idea. He Googled the manufacturer and located a Customer Service email address. He sent them an email with a picture of the coat and button, including a measurement. A few emails and about two weeks later, he received a replacement button. The company was so service-oriented that they even thanked him for thanking them.

My friend, on the other hand, decided to go through the salesperson who had sold her the coat, a person with whom she has an ongoing relationship. Her rationale was that because of that relationship it would be an easy mission. Nice thought, which can work sometimes, but incorrect in this case. This salesperson started working with store staff—managers, merchandise managers, buyers. Her salesfriend got in touch with the store contacts who had access to the manufacturer. It was unclear who was doing what but they seemed to be falling over each other in an effort to locate the tag and snaps. But there was my friend, twelve weeks out and into spring, and no tag, no snaps.

What's wrong with this picture?

1. My friend was dealing through the store and a known contact, which can sometimes be productive. But it hadn't been productive in this case. As time passed, she was less likely to have her tag and snaps, especially since the hunt had extended into the next season. *If you're moving along without progress, try something different.*

2. She hadn't located the person in the store or within the store's National management who had the relationship

with someone specific at the manufacturer. Who's in charge here? Who has the clout?

3. We also didn't know if anyone was taking responsibility for locating the tag and snaps on the manufacturer end.

4. The quest for the tag was probably impeding the quest for the snaps. It is more likely for a manufacturer to stock extra snaps than it is for them to stock extra tags. I don't understand why she wanted the tag, but she wouldn't give it up—maybe she has a tag jar like my button jar? Too weird—I don't want to know. There was a Grand Ole Opry personality, Minnie Pearl, who used to wear her tags on the outside of her hats. I don't think that my friend was channeling her inner Minnie Pearl, but...

What could be done differently?

1. My friend could talk to her salesfriend to get the name of the person in the store who was dealing with the manufacturer. She could then make contact with that person directly to understand exactly what was going on.

2. From what my friend could gather, all communication between the store and the manufacturer was through email. *When there is an extended time lag from the start of the issue and email isn't resolving the problem, it's time to pick up the phone.*

3. She could drop the Mission Impossible on the tag search and focus on what was important—the snaps. *Too many sidebars can distract from the real issue.*

When you compare the two quests—Howard's button quest and my friend's snap and tag quest—look at the process and the outcome. Howard went the simple route and he has his replacement button. My friend was hoping that her relationship and focus on special contacts would get her what she wanted. Her method wasn't working this time. She was still waiting. Hopefully, she wouldn't lose a snap while she waited, but the longer she waited, the less likely it was that she'd get her extras—at this point, she was probably screwed unless she went a different route.

If your method for resolution isn't working, try a different method. And, sometimes it's better to think horses rather than zebras when you hear hoof beats—there are times when the simplest course of action is the one that works.

FROM REFRIGERATOR TO TOILET—A TALE OF HOME REPAIR

THERE'S MORE THAN ONE WAY

Howard and I are getting old. How do I know this? I found a few new gray hairs recently. Howard's rallying call is "Where did I put my reading glasses?" The little annoyances that come with age are nothing compared to the aggravation of dealing with an aging home, where it seems that almost every week, there is something that needs repair or replacement.

We remodeled our kitchen a few years ago, or so it seemed. One day, I opened the refrigerator and found a chunk of frost on the inside of the freezer door. Not enough to make a snowman, but it certainly needed to be addressed before we had a refrigerator meltdown. When I called the appliance repair contractor, they asked for a serial number. As I looked for the serial number, I saw that the date was marked 1992. Did we really redo the kitchen that long ago? I guess so. Time flies when you're in denial.

At the same time that I was having my refrigerator problem, a friend also had a problem with a different brand and had to use a different repair service. His refrigerator had stopped producing ice. Let's look at the two different repair experiences and two different ways of resolving a problem.

My repair service was very user-friendly. The repairman told me that there was probably an air leak, and a replacement gasket would probably take care of it. He had to order the gasket and would return to install it. I thought that while he was there, I would mention that some pieces of ice had black flecks in them. The technician thought that it would be a good idea to replace the icemaker as well. I had a good feel for the company and knew that the refrigerator was old, so I had him replace it, even though I didn't have the technical expertise to know whether this was the right answer. The black flecks disappeared after the repair, so he was right. I wouldn't have called for repair on that issue alone, but it was a good idea to have all issues addressed at once. *Be aware that for every trip regarding a*

107

new issue on most home maintenance services, you will have a new trip charge. This can range from about $60 to $95. It's better to deal with as much as possible on one visit.

My repairman came back and installed the gasket. The total charge on all services was about $300. After about a week, I noticed that frost was starting to form again. I called the appliance repair company. The repairman returned and added silicone to the inside of the gasket. What a mess! He was about to leave when I noticed little silicone balls all over the edging of the gasket and on the floor. They looked like blobs of white freckles –yuck! I asked him to clean it off to make it neat. He did that. No charge and all issues were fixed—or so I thought.

A few days later, I saw frost. I called for repair again. When I spoke with the technician, he told me that he would have to charge this time, since I had asked him to remove the silicone. At this point, I needed to talk to someone else. I hadn't asked the repairman to remove the silicone but simply to make it neat, I shouldn't be charged, and the problem still wasn't fixed. I needed silicone insulation, not silicone mess.

Time to move up the ladder—I asked for the Service Manager. He agreed to come out himself, without charge, and make it right. I later found that the original technician was good, but newer and young. (I already knew the young part.) The manager was more seasoned, understood the sloppy silicone problem and returned to fix it. Before he could return for the frost problem, however, the icemaker had stopped working. When the manager came to the house, he added silicone (neatly) and told me that the icemaker issue was a coincidence, not a result of the replacement, and I needed a new valve. He seemed to know what he was doing, and the visit charge was only for the valve replacement—about $100, so I told him to fix it. I later found that he was right because the icemaker has been fine ever since.

But the frost continued, though much less. I've lost count of the number of times the technician returned, but he was responsive. I finally dealt with the owner, who assured me that there would be no charge as they made the adjustments, because their repairs are warrantied for a year. They were so good that they even called me a few days after each repair to see if everything was working okay. I got lucky in finding such a good service.

On the other hand, my friend didn't have a good experience with his refrigerator repair. He had to use another service because he had a different brand of refrigerator, and my service was not authorized to repair his brand. Repair services are often small businesses, not large corporations. This has its pros and cons. If they are good, that's great, because you usually get good personalized service. If they aren't good, it can be difficult to get to the right person to resolve the problem—in a small business, there simply aren't many staff options.

Unfortunately, my friend had real problems with his service company. His serviceman came out five times, but never resolved the problem fully. Each time, my friend was given a different explanation, and charges added up to $509 in total—$95 for the initial service call, plus a variety of charges each time they returned. Finally, the freezer started making ice, but it wouldn't produce crushed ice as it should have and the dispenser wasn't perfect. He could live with this, but it wasn't a full resolution and he wasn't happy.

The final insult was that the repair service told him that he now needed a new motor, and that there would be another charge for it. This didn't make sense after so many visits. It would seem that somewhere in the diagnostics and over the course of five visits, this should have come up before my friend spent over $500 in repairs.

What could he do to resolve the problem? I suggested that he contact the owner. This didn't work—the owner said that from his review, they had considered a new motor from the beginning. My friend said that no one ever mentioned a motor. The owner wouldn't budge on rebating any charges or coming out again without charging.

Without clear oversight over this small business, my friend thought that he should contact the Better Business Bureau. I didn't think that this would yield immediate results. Although the BBB does good things, the only action that they could take would be to accept a complaint, and if anyone inquired, the complaint would be on file. Registering a complaint wouldn't resolve my friend's problem. I suggested that he contact the Executive Office of the manufacturer of the refrigerator as an alternative. My logic: if the manufacturer authorized the dealer for service, the manufacturer could have some clout. Unfortunately, that didn't work. He reached an apathetic Executive assistant who didn't do anything. I would have pushed on to find someone more responsive in the Executive Headquarters, but my friend was ready to pull his hair out and gave up on this path.

His next idea was a good one. He called his credit card company, and put a "dispute" on the repair charges. Good for him! The credit card company fell into the middle of a "he said/she said" situation. They weren't in a position to know who was right. However, in an effort to provide good service to a customer who had been with them for a long time, they offered a compromise. They were willing to credit his account for $350. I thought that this seemed reasonable. My friend's final tally for service went down to a little over $150. It wasn't a perfect solution, but it was something. Remember that without any repair activity, he would have paid $95 for the service call alone, and he does say that his icemaker is usable.

Two similar problems—two different resolutions. With my problem, going higher in a responsive company worked; with my friend's problem, thinking creatively worked.

But, there was another kink in my repair story. I needed a new toilet because I had refrigerator problems. How did I get from refrigerator to toilet?

When my repairman fixed the icemaker, he had to turn off the water to the refrigerator. In doing this, the 27 year- old shutoff valve snapped off—not his fault; it was old. He couldn't fix it, so I had to call the plumber.

When I called the plumbing service, I reached the owner and asked for an estimate. *Always ask for an estimate at the start—it gives you a frame of reference if you have pricing issues later.* The owner told me that the repair would be in the $130 to $160 range. He sent out a plumber and a helper. They fixed the valve.

In order to repair the valve they had to shut off the water and open all of the faucets. When they opened one of the bathtub faucets, I noticed that it was a little loose. Remember that I've said that it's better to address multiple issues on one visit to avoid extra visit charges? I still stand by that, but this is where my plumbing problems started. Since the faucet was loose and I also realized that a toilet needed to be caulked, I had him do those minor repairs as well. The final tally for the day was $291.

The charge seemed high and I didn't understand why—with the original estimate of $130 to $160, plus five minutes for the helper to tighten the faucet and 10 minutes for the plumber to caulk, why was the charge suddenly that much higher? I talked to the plumber about this but paid the bill anyway, thinking that I would talk to the owner, who had given me the original estimate. I trusted him, having dealt with him before. My thinking was that they had come out quickly, did the work, and deserved to be paid. Paying him at the time of service was right; paying the full amount was wrong.

When Howard came home, he pointed out that the faucet was appropriately tight, but now turned 360 degrees, when it wasn't supposed to do that. My mistake—now I have two problems. I didn't check everything before they left, and I paid the full bill rather than making a partial payment while I checked on the pricing.

I spoke with the owner. He's a responsive guy, but a bit disorganized. He did come out to fix the faucet. Addressing the bill, while he'd been in the business long enough to know charges, he wanted to figure out the cost by computer to be exact. I would have been okay with a ballpark reasonable figure. He was having problems with his computer service, which was delaying my refund. On the overcharge, after about three weeks of emails and phone calls, I finally proposed that he trade a new toilet seat, including the installation cost, for the overcharge on the last visit. He liked that idea. Overcharge resolved.

When the plumber installed the new toilet seat, I remembered my rule—take care of everything at once to avoid new service charges. So, I asked him to tighten the toilet in the hall bathroom—a toilet that they had installed, but it was a little bit wobbly. He tightened it and left. I thought we were finished with plumbing for now. I was wrong.

The first time that we used the tightened toilet, it cracked right along the base where the plumber had tightened the bolt. Obviously, he had tightened it too much.

What to do now? It was a weekend, and I wrote an email to the plumbing company with the subject line "HELP!!" On Monday, the plumber called to say that I would need a new toilet. I didn't want a new toilet, but I had no choice. The owner was out of town for the week, so that the estimate wasn't from the horse's mouth. The plumber said that he would take $100 off of the price when I pointed out that his tightening caused the crack. He couldn't argue with my logic, not to mention the other recent issues—the last overcharge, the faucet error. But he didn't budge on the price. We scheduled the appointment. An hour after he was supposed to arrive, I called to find out where he was. Somehow, I had dropped off of the schedule. Add this to the list of screw-ups.

When the plumber replaced the toilet, I told him that I was paying him half of the cost, pending discussion with the owner. He was okay with that. When the owner came back and heard the story, he was fine with the payment. In this last situation, *I had learned from my former error in paying a questionable bill in full. Better for me to hold back when the bill is unclear, rather than chase after the plumber for reimbursement. It's always better to hold the cards, as long as you're fair and have a good reason.*

I hope that we don't need any more repairs in the near future. I'm sure that the hope is only a pipe dream.

EXPERT OR MYTH?

CONVERSATIONS WITH MY CAR

There is an anthropomorphic quality to my car. This has been going on for years. Every car we've owned had a unique personality and communicated in quirky ways. The challenge was to learn the car's language. What was it trying to tell me?

Our first car was Martian-like. There was no way to predict its behavior. It had cute turn signals, where a series of lights would stream to let people know whether we were going left or right. For no reason, the lights would periodically falter and fixing them was always an adventure.

During a vacation, we went to visit a friend who was finishing graduate school in a remote upstate college town. After a few days, the starter motor died for no apparent reason. Not wanting to trust an unknown mechanic, and not wanting to be stuck in Podunk forever, we had a garage get the motor going, but we couldn't turn it off. Howard waited in the car with the motor running, while I packed so that we could return to our trusted home mechanic. With the pressure to vamoose and the motor running, we felt like Bonnie and Clyde, but without the machine guns.

We later owned the car from hell with the bad carburetor that made us stall all the time. Unfortunately, this happened before Lemon Laws. We were also young and inexperienced, so we tolerated more than we should have. If this happened today, I would have had a new car or a decent fix by going up the chain of command within the car manufacturer when the dealer wasn't helpful—Lemon Law or no Lemon Law. Instead, in those days, I developed a long and close relationship with a mechanic near work, who would take the car, drive me to work, and get the car going until the next stall out.

One day when I dropped Howard at work and tried to drive on to my office, I stalled in the middle of a major intersection with a bus behind me. I'd had it! I got out of the car and started to walk away while the bus driver cursed and screamed at me.

"I'm done!" I said to my horrified husband as he stood on the sidewalk watching me abandon the car. People on the street gawked and probably thought that I must be nuts. Little did they know—it was the car that was nuts, not me. It was just driving me there—or, more accurately, making me nuts by not driving me anywhere. As we argued about whether it was the fault of the driver or the car, Howard got into the car, finally got it going and realized that it was a car glitch, not my fault. Once again, my mechanic and I were back in a close relationship. We finally got rid of the car, but the memory of its personality lingered for far too long.

I've had my current car longer than any I've ever owned. I love it, but it, too, has its quirks. I was driving to work one day, when I heard a sudden beep. I didn't know what was happening. Then, I noticed that there was a symbol lit on the dashboard. It looked like an upside down light bulb with a giant X through it. Why couldn't it just speak English? A few weeks later, my car actually did speak English, telling me that my right tipped headlight was out—it said it right on the dash. I had no idea what a "tipped" headlight was. With that first beep and picture, I guessed that I probably had a burnt out headlight or brake light. I drove to the dealer immediately. Jake in the Service Department looked at the headlights, had me hit the brake lights, but couldn't see a problem.

EXPERT OR MYTH?

He told me that I could bring the car in for service, it could take hours, because they had to figure out what was wrong, and if it was a headlight, they had to pretty much deconstruct the car to reach the headlight. I made the appointment.

Wait a minute. Why was I taking the car in if Jake couldn't see anything that was obviously wrong? When I got to work, I went above the Service technician to the Service Manager. When I told him my story, he told me that he would be glad to have his team check my car, but the likelihood of finding anything was minimal, since there was no obvious light out and the beep and picture had stopped. He explained that they would hook the car up to a computer and if the computer didn't tell them that something was wrong—which was the probable scenario—there was nothing that they could do. His suggestion was to just wait and see what happened next, especially since there was no danger issue.

I did just what he said to do—I waited. I have since found that my car periodically talks to me. It beeps and shows a picture of the upside down light bulb with the red X, and when I notice and turn off the car and re-start it, I'm back to normal.

When you're looking for expert advice, make sure that you really are talking to an expert. If it sounds funky and smells funky, it's probably funky—and wrong. I saved aggravation and an unnecessary car service. My car and I are still on speaking terms—at least for now.

EXPERT OR NOT

Vacations never come frequently enough or last long enough. Why does the anticipation remain for such a long time, but the time away flies by so quickly? Maybe my next project could be to stop time—nah, scientists can't do it, so this is something that I can't fix.

We usually start to plan a spring vacation in December. When we are in the throes of winter doldrums, the activity of planning an escape for the spring makes me see visions of the promise of good things to come. However, as with many projects, there are hassles in the process.

For a few years, we used a travel agent for major trips. Initially, she was very helpful, suggesting hotels and making arrangements, all based on her experience in the industry. After a few trips, she was less helpful and we found that we could take care of things on our own.

On one trip, we were going to Vienna and Paris. We had been to both cities before. In Vienna, we were going to stay at a wonderful hotel where we had stayed previously and which had been recommended by the travel agent. This time her price quote was rather high. *What do you do when something seems off? Check it yourself.* We went online and found that this hotel had a deal where you could get one free night with a three night stay. Why wasn't that part of our arrangement? We went back to the travel agent, who told us that this didn't apply to our room level, and the fact that we had a package that included breakfast also made us ineligible for the promotion.

Her answer didn't feel right. Maybe she was correct, but wouldn't it seem that for a returning guest staying in an upgraded room, there should be some type of a promotion, if not that specific deal? So, we checked it ourselves. Howard called the company that owns the hotel. He found that even with our room upgrade and breakfast, there was a special promotion, and he was able to book the same room at $1000 less than the travel agent's booking. Major savings! When we told the travel agent, she stumbled all over herself to find excuses for her lapse, telling us that although we did get the lower rate, they probably made an error. I doubt it.

The flight issue was the next problem. When we go between cities, we only use a one-way ticket because we come home from the last port of call. The first time we did this, the cost of a one-way ticket was very high. The travel agent found that a round trip ticket was significantly cheaper. She had the good idea to book the round trip flight, and throw away the return ticket. We've been doing this ever since thanks to her ingenuity. However, although she had a few good ideas, on the whole, she wasn't so helpful. Like the time that we had to book seats on the plane between Vienna and Paris.

She said that there was no way to obtain the seat assignments in advance. We didn't like the idea of having seats assigned at the airport, since this could lead to glitches. Isn't the point of vacation to stay clear of glitches? We tried to obtain the seats on our own, but couldn't do it either. The day before we were to fly to Paris, we decided to ask the hotel concierge in Vienna whether he could do anything to obtain the seat assignments in advance. He was more knowledgeable than the travel agent, realizing that the airline based in Paris partnered with the airline in Vienna, so the seat assignment could be made through this partner airline. He did that, which saved us probable aggravation at the airport. The travel agent had years of experience—she should have known about the partnering or done a little more research to find out.

We were starting to have problems with her attentiveness in other areas. On a trip to California, we needed a rental car. We usually make our own arrangements for short and uncomplicated trips like this one—simple airfare, we knew the hotel where we wanted to stay, and we needed a rental car. We let the travel agent book the trip, thinking that it would be easier and that she might find a decent deal.

For the car rental, we have a professional association discount with the rental company. We gave the travel agent the information and let her do the booking. When we returned the car, we found that the bill was $320 for four days. That's $80 per day for a basic compact car and included the normal discount. This seemed excessive. Earlier in the summer while driving my own car, someone backed into me in a parking lot. When I had a loaner car while my car was being repaired, I had a basic compact car, and the daily charge was $26. I know that car rental companies discount for insurers, but even doubling the discounted $26 rate would only be $52 per day. The travel agent's booking got us a rate that was way out of line. Nothing special was going on—it was the end of September, no special holidays. I just didn't understand this excessive bill and hoped that it might be incorrect.

Since the travel agent had made the arrangements, it seemed appropriate to have her deal with the problem. It was not an unreasonable assumption to think that she might have some type of direct line to a dedicated Customer Service area. Since she receives a commission for the booking, why shouldn't she complete the work? I emailed her with the problem issue and asked her to check it out. She said that it did seem a little high and that she would look into it. After a week without a response, I emailed her again. She said that she was told that there were fewer cars available at that time and this was the reason for the high charge. She had given up too easily. Another email—I told her that regardless of availability, with the reservation made well in advance, the charge was still excessive and asked her to let her contact know that the rental company had a very dissatisfied and (formerly?) loyal customer who would be willing to look at other rental companies for the future if they couldn't be more reasonable. I asked her to let them know that I expected some type of credit to my charge account, not a future discount. (Note that I used the word "expected," not "hoped for" or some other less strong word.) This request was based on several issues:

1. We had never had a daily charge in that range, regardless of any complicating factors.

2. Based on my summer loaner experience, this charge was way out of line, and

3. There should be some consideration of customer loyalty, since we were "Preferred Customers" who had a history with the company.

Armed with my guidance, the travel agent went back to her contact. After six weeks, she came back with the rental company's offer. They would offer a $25 "courtesy" rebate. Of course, this was insufficient on a $320 charge. I realized that I had gone as far as I could go with the travel agent, who either wasn't very effective, wasn't very invested in a reasonable resolution or just didn't care. At this point, it was easier to do it myself.

I went on the Internet, Googled the Corporate Headquarters for the rental company, and located a Corporate phone number. In my most authoritative voice, I asked for the President's assistant. I reached Mary in the President's Office, who directed me to the Corporate Executive Customer Service line. This was a small area dedicated to escalated issues, manned by two people, one of whom was out of the office. I emailed the issue to one of them, Joe, who responded saying that he couldn't make the adjustment, but included me in an email to another resource, who was supposed to get back to me the next day. When I didn't receive a call from Joe's contact the next day, I called back to Mary in the Office of the President. She was patient and nice, but she did say that the Executive Customer Service area receives many calls. (Prodding gently, I commented, "And complaints?") She asked me to leave a message for Joe and said that she would email him, as well. Later that day, I received a message from the area manager in California. Although I returned his call, I hadn't heard back from him within two days. I left another message, politely noting my concern about the amount of time this was taking for such a simple issue that I hoped could be easily resolved. Within an hour, I had a call back.

Frank, the area manager, listened to all of my reasons for feeling that the charge was too high and that the $25 courtesy credit was not sufficient to address the problem. His response was that we had traveled during a time when there was a high car demand and they had fewer cars. Like hotels and airlines, when there is less supply, the charges go up. I told him that I understood that, but that the increase was excessive. I noted my summer loaner example. I added that we had never paid in that range in all of our prior bookings and that if they weren't interested in my business, there were other rental companies for future business—all stated politely but firmly. I also told him that I understand the laws of supply and demand, but that *there is a difference between supply and demand versus price gouging.*

Finally, realizing that I wouldn't let this go, he asked what I thought would be appropriate. I replied that an additional $50 would demonstrate his company's good will. At this point, while I wanted a fairer price, I felt it was okay to lowball, since I wanted to prove a point and didn't feel that the issue was worth further haggling. He agreed to the credit. I was satisfied. When my credit card bill arrived, there was a credit for $43.87. Why $43.87? While the difference between this amount and the promised $50 was not a big deal, I was curious about what type of Corporate mumbo jumbo created this weird refund amount. I called Frank. He was as confused as I was—he had put through a $50 credit. He offered to send me a coupon for a $25 discount on our next rental as compensation for my time and the company's odd calculation. Nice gesture and adequate compensation.

There are several lessons here, comparing the two approaches to the problem (the travel agent's and mine)—as well as a few pointers to avoid the problem for future:

1. Although this booking could have worked out fine, it would have been better if we had booked the car rental ourselves and had the pricing information up front. If we were given the same out of line price, it would have been better to address it on the front end, so that we would either have been able to negotiate a better price or gone to another rental company. This would have avoided surprises and aggravation.

2. It was a logical assumption to believe that the travel agent had connections that would allow her to resolve the problem. In many businesses, agents are connected to dedicated representatives or areas of a resource company, so they should have contacts to fix problems. With the right connection and a focused, firm approach, she may have accomplished more. Or, maybe she didn't have a good contact and felt that it wasn't worth her time to find one. It should have been worth her time—she was making a commission and we were dissatisfied clients.

3. Since we had dealt with the travel agent by email, my guess is that she was dealing with her contact by email as well. *Email is not always the best way to achieve an objective. You can't hear a voice, and tone is very important to understand the meaning behind words. Email is okay for basics, but it's not the best tool for negotiation.*

4. There were several actions that I took that the travel agent did not take. First, I looked for an area of the rental company that would be likely to respond to a customer issue. Customer Service could have been a first line contact, but, having seen little from my travel agent's efforts, I thought that I would be dealing with a low-level person who would take some rote company policy position rather than recognizing my issue. A first-line contact would probably not have enough authority to be flexible, especially after a small credit had been issued. Although I could have gone to a supervisor, enough routine channels were exhausted through the travel agent, so it was appropriate for me to go to Executive. Internet research using "Corporate Headquarters" got me there. I also wasn't going to allow excessive time to elapse. *It is always better to deal with an issue quickly.* Sometimes, it does take time for someone to get back to you. However, the six week lag time for the response from the travel agent's contact was excessive and enough to allow me to push for responsiveness. The lack of responsiveness initially added credence to my argument that attention to customer issues wasn't great.

5. My argument was clear and sound: my longtime history with the company, the fact that there had never been charges in this range, my analogy to the loaner experience when my own car was being repaired, the point that there is a difference between charging more based on supply and demand versus price gouging, and the fact that there are other options for me other than their company. These were all reasonable points to support my request.

6. While I could have asked for a little more of a refund, I was clear that I was being reasonable, which added to my credibility.

7. My persistence was a factor in obtaining a reasonable response. The travel agent waited too long for the rental company to get back to her and didn't prod them. Prodding was a very useful tool in my resolution of the issue.

I'm not sure what was going on with the travel agent. Was she complacent, just doing the basics to bring in her commission? Were we overly impressed by the round trip airfare idea? After the initial interactions, we were accomplishing what she failed to accomplish. Generally, relying on expertise is a good way to go. But, if the expert no longer seems to be effective, it's time to move on. *If an expert is helpful, that's great. If not, find another expert, or do it yourself.*

CORPORATE GIANTS—HOW TO CLIMB THE BEANSTALK

CORPORATE GIANTS—HOW TO CLIMB THE BEANSTALK

I have issues with large corporations. Some are consumer friendly, but many are not. The ease or difficulty level usually depends on Corporate culture and policies, as well as the specific people with whom you are dealing. Bigger isn't always better. Many corporations can be top-heavy, with Corporate policy often neglecting customer needs. While this can be a problem, there are still ways to accomplish a goal and obtain good customer service by making your way to the right person or department. You can find good contacts who can make customer friendly decisions. Unless you live in a cave, it's impossible to live in a world where you won't have to deal with large corporations. So, here are a few examples of how to make them work for you.

MORTGAGE SLEIGHT OF HAND

Tenacity is key to problem resolution. You can often experience serious roadblocks when a company tries to avoid resolving issues in a customer-friendly manner. If they think that they can make you go away, believe me, they will often try to do that. Consider my mortgage issue:

Howard and I decided to take a small mortgage. We went back to the bank that held our last mortgage. Howard contacted a local mortgage sales person, Jeff, and they agreed on terms. The initial contacts were over the phone. We had to send in a $375 deposit, and the contracts and other documents would be forthcoming. After a significant delay, the documents arrived—with the wrong terms. Howard had agreed to a 15 year mortgage at 5%. The documents arrived with a 30 year mortgage and a 5.5% rate. Howard emailed Jeff and pointed out the discrepancy. Because we had a mortgage with this bank before and had no problems, it was not unreasonable to send the deposit based on the phone interaction. Wrong! *Afterthought and warning—never send a deposit without a document, no matter how trustworthy the other party seems.*

When we were dealing with the bank previously, we were dealing with the area that handles the day-to-day operations for existing mortgages. Sales is a whole different arena. If Jeff had balked at sending the terms prior to receiving the deposit, we would have had the clear message that something wasn't right and wouldn't have followed through. Lesson learned.

Now, with a discrepancy about terms, Howard started to document his interactions with Jeff. He sent Jeff an email stating that they had agreed on different terms than what Jeff had delivered, noting the delay in obtaining the documents, and stated that Jeff must either honor the original terms, or refund the deposit. Jeff's response: "I will do neither." Big mistake, Jeff! (And notice, he didn't argue what had been discussed, but simply decided that the terms would be his terms alone.)

There was a little more email correspondence, but no movement. In order to expedite the mortgage, we decided to go to a different bank, since it was becoming obvious that arguing further was going to be time consuming and fruitless. We were able to locate another bank very easily and even obtained a slightly better rate.

Initially, we thought that the $375 deposit was lost. Of course, I couldn't let that slide. I decided to pursue a refund. Jeff had acted on bad faith, had stonewalled us in our initial attempt to rectify the situation, and had acted dishonestly and unprofessionally. At the time that we were applying for the mortgage, the US government had been dealing with the mortgage debacle of 2007. Banks were not institutions with good public image. I kept this in mind as I worked on a strategy.

The most appropriate first step was to go to Jeff's manager. I located that person by calling the local branch of the bank where Howard had initially contacted Jeff. We could have gone to Jeff's direct supervisor. That person may or may not have been helpful. However, since I was dealing with a highly regulated industry—banking—I felt that the decision maker would have to be higher up the ladder. I was also asking for something that was probably outside of a routine request, and wanted to ensure that someone in a significant enough position would be aware of Jeff's behavior so that it could be addressed.

CORPORATE GIANTS—HOW TO CLIMB THE BEANSTALK

David was Jeff's manager. I left a voicemail message for him, simply stating that I was calling about a problem with a mortgage and wanted to speak with him to resolve it. I didn't know if David was more honest than Jeff. Was he aware of Jeff's style of doing business? If so, did he sanction it? Did he direct Jeff to operate in this manner? Or, was he more aware of banking regulations, customer service, etc.? Because I had no sense of David, I left him just enough information to tantalize him into calling me back. If I was calling about a mortgage, this could be new business. If I had left greater detail in this situation, I risked not getting a call back.

David called back immediately. I explained the situation. He was obnoxious. His tone was bullying and unyielding. In my argument, I pointed out that Jeff clearly misled Howard, and the language in his email ("I will do neither") underscored his dishonesty. David didn't flinch at the dishonesty and continued on the same path. I pointed out that we had no choice other than going to another bank, which hadn't been our original intention. He attempted to bully me into staying with his bank, saying that he would now meet the original terms. I was clear that it was too late at that point and trust had been lost. David was clear that he would not rebate the deposit. I then asked for the contact information to the bank's Executive Department at the National level. His response: "No!" His response to my position that a reimbursement needed to occur: "It's not happening." This terse, stonewalling response and David's failure to recognize an ethical lapse, a customer service lapse, and the possibility of a legal breach all led me to continue my fight. I became equally terse and clear with David. I told him that if he thought that he could block my path to Executive, he was mistaken, and that his behavior would be another issue to address with Executive when I reached them. I also promised him that I would be in touch with the appropriate authority. Little did he know that I always keep my promises.

It would have been nice to have a handy number to call. I could have randomly called a branch of the bank. In many cases, local staff can give out a National Customer Service number. While these numbers are sometimes helpful, sometimes they are not, especially for an issue like this one where oversight and the state of banking at that time were larger issues.

I Googled the Corporate Headquarters of the bank, looking for a Public Relations area. I have found that this can be a good way to locate the appropriate Executive area because if there is a problem, Public Relations is concerned about the company's public image. It's in their best interest to have a problem resolved. When I spoke with Public Relations, I explained that I was a customer (or would have been), that I had a problem with a mortgage representative, and that I would like to speak with someone at a level high enough to resolve the issue, hoping to avoid having to go to Federal oversight.

Holding out the Federal reporting possibility was a good strategy to get their attention. While this would have been appropriate at any point in time, especially with the banking and mortgage mess that was occurring nationally at the time, there was additional jeopardy for the bank if this turned out to be a government oversight issue. *It is important to be clear—you can't just threaten. The person you are speaking with has to understand that you will follow through if necessary. My tone said that I would.*

I was given the number to the Executive Resolutions area. This was a call center, but a small call center for higher level problems. Initially, I spoke with a savvy representative. When I explained the issue, he agreed to follow up with Jeff and David. Neither of them responded to his initial phone messages. Given their sleazy behavior, this wasn't surprising. On the other hand, it was a bit disconcerting that that they weren't responding to a contact from Executive Resolutions, which was many levels above them.

I continued to call the Executive representative every few days. He finally decided that this needed further escalation and sent the issue to the manager of the Executive area. She tried to contact the Regional Manager over both Jeff and David. The Regional Manager didn't respond either. Lack of response to many outreaches underscored my position. I also learned a little (very little) about mortgages and banking in the process. Although I was in Executive, they couldn't simply refund our deposit without sign off by the local Mortgage Sales Department that had originally accepted the deposit. I found that this really was a part of the Federal banking regulation. So, as much as they wanted to simply write me a check, they couldn't. As this process dragged out over the course of a few months, I was more determined that I would not only obtain the refund, but that I would ensure that sanctions were levied on the Regional people involved. *I made sure that the Executive manager followed up by continuing to call her every few days or at least once a week.* Although she did continue her efforts to reach the appropriate parties, she wasn't getting anywhere.

Finally, when I pointed out that I appreciated her assistance, but that it was unacceptable for Regional to continue to ignore Executive, she took this to a higher level in the Executive Department. She reached Kate, who was actually located in the Office of the President. Kate recognized the shady and evasive behavior at the Regional and Local end and she began to copy all of her emails to much higher level people—Vice Presidents, Operations Executives, etc. I finally received my reimbursement, with an apology and an assurance (which I do believe was real) that this incident would be documented so that higher level people would sanction Jeff, David, and their Regional Manager.

In this situation, if I hadn't been tenacious, I would have lost the battle. Typically, deposits such as this one aren't rebated. *However, I had my clear argument and I had documentation of bad faith because I saved Jeff's emails.* Jeff's superiors shot themselves in the collective foot by refusing to return Executive messages—underscoring the fact that my story was an accurate account of a disingenuous operation. I was totally unfazed by David's stonewalling attempt and determined to push past that. I don't think that he expected that I could do this. If I hadn't continued to follow up closely and push through the Executive chain, despite the bank being supportive of my argument, the obstacles created by the Regional people probably would have worn out Executive staff. It was very clear that worn out or not, I wasn't stopping until I had a proper resolution.

Too often, people like Jeff and David are allowed to intimidate, mislead, and bully consumers, often because no one else knows about it. This is simply unacceptable, and as you can see, there are ways to attack this position. As a footnote, this bank, among others, was later fined by the government for other shady mortgage practices. If you wait long enough, you'll usually see something like this happen. If you've had an experience of this magnitude, there's a pretty good chance that you're not alone.

CABLE WARS—THE SHOT IN THE FOOT

I shot myself in the foot while standing on my principles.

In the world of cable, figuring out the best prices, how to get decent service and how to remain sane through it all adds up to a small war. Since I'm not a fan of behemoth corporations, I decided that I wouldn't be taken hostage by one large corporation. To avoid falling into that scenario, Howard and I used two cable services—one for TV and a competitor for phone and Internet. It took me too long to realize that this wasn't accomplishing my goal of avoiding having one company take advantage of me. It was actually costing me more, so that I was allowing two companies to take advantage of me. How could I resolve this without getting rooked?

We'd had problems with both companies over the years. At one point, we had problems with TV reception. After many calls and repair visits, the cable company finally ran a new underground cable on our property. The reception still wasn't great. About a year later, after a torrential rain, we had no picture—only static. When I called for service, they found that the company had run the cable, but never connected it to the main box! Through escalated contacts, I negotiated a year of free cable as pay back for that lapse.

On the telephone side, we have two lines. We added the second line when Cory and Tracy were teenagers, before the age of cell phones. We never bothered to get rid of the second line when they were in college; it wasn't very expensive and seemed to be insurance in case of a problem on Line 1. We could use it for DSL, but rarely used it otherwise. Years down the pike, I had a spike in the charges on Line 2. When I called to find out why, I was told that this was due to "under usage". Really—I couldn't make that up. An escalated contact removed the extra charge, gave me a courtesy credit for my aggravation and time, and put a flag on the account so that it wouldn't happen again.

Over the years, I learned to work with both companies, resolving problems by finding good escalated contacts. When problems arose, I could usually get them fixed quickly. But, it took me too long to realize that the cost of service from two companies was too high. We were receiving two bills. Yet, even with that, I thought that I was winning because I could always pit one company against the other, with each company knowing that I had service through the other company and that neither one had all of my business. I was wrong—I wasn't winning. Or, it was a pyrrhic victory—I was nobody's fool but my own and I was paying top dollar for that privilege.

My wake-up call came with new cost changes. The promotion for each company usually lasted for a year. If I didn't call them to find out about new promotional pricing for the next year, I would have seen even higher bills. How did I know this? I knew it because one day when I opened the TV bill, I saw a large increase. When I called to find out why, I was told that my promotion had expired. *From that point on, I marked my calendar a few weeks before the yearly promotional price was to end, and called to negotiate a better rate.* This worked for a while. But it was a nuisance, and after a few years, both companies were becoming tougher about negotiating the rates. When the TV company reduced their promotional period to six months, I decided that this was unacceptable. I was able to convince my escalated contact to extend it for the year instead. But, any value and issue resolution was contingent upon the contacts I was working with. If they left, I knew that I would work with a new contact to achieve something reasonable. But it was getting more difficult and more irritating. Not that I would ever give up. But, there had to be a better way. Serendipity found that better way.

One day, we suddenly lost phone service. When I contacted the telephone company, I got their standard response. They hoped to have my phone service restored within four days from the time of outage. Four days! No way. *I used my escalated contacts who dealt with bills to find an escalated contact in the Service area.* That worked well. Within a day we had phone service. About a year later, we lost service again. This time, I went right to the escalated Service contacts and had service restored within two hours.

After this last incident, the phone company decided to be proactive. A couple of weeks after the last outage, I received a call from someone in the company's Executive area, who had seen that we'd had phone problems twice in too short a period of time. She saw that our wiring was old. She offered a free upgrade to fiber optics and service at a better rate than the rate that we were paying at the time. Encouraged that the company was trying to make me happy and keep my business, I asked about a package that would include TV, phone and computer. She found a two year plan—not six months, not one year, but two years—that would cost me half of what I was paying by staying with both companies. I liked that! But, I did point out that there could be a "gotcha" so that when it came time to renew, they could significantly raise the price.

I don't like "gotchas". My contact agreed that I had a point but also agreed to work with me. Why should I trust her, and what if she wasn't with the company in two years? I trusted her because she was incredibly responsive, returning calls immediately, resolving the glitches in the change, and worked with me to remove the dumb charges that shouldn't be there—one time connection fee, one time activation fee, etc. And, I had enough escalated contacts and would push hard enough if I needed new ones so that I felt okay about making the change. Also, remember that we're still wired for the other TV company, so we can switch back if we decide at some point that the new arrangement doesn't meet our needs.

    Before making the commitment to the company, I called an escalated contact at the competitor company to give them the opportunity to win me over. Their options were not as enticing as the first company's and they didn't offer adjustments that would keep my business. I guess that this meant that my escalated contacts at my new carrier were better than those at the other carrier, and the business model at that time was more customer friendly with the new carrier, too.

    So, here I am, with all of my services at half the price that I was paying before and with the knowledge that I still have choices if I need them. Surprisingly, my old company misses me and has tried to court me back. Periodically, they send me love letters with new promotional offers. They use their affectionate pet name for me—"Occupant".

    I think that my current company loves me—at least for now. And, I learned that having the upper hand doesn't mean that I need to have a hole in my foot.

FLYING UNDER THE RADAR

Airlines hold a special place in the Corporate world. With deregulation and mergers creating mega-airlines, the deck is usually stacked in their favor. They know it and they take advantage of it. They can be behemoths with rigid rules that are not easy to navigate. But, at times, I have been able to achieve a few major coups.

Tracy had flown back and forth to college for four years on one airline, the predominant carrier for her route. The planes that they used for this particular route were part of a subsidiary of the airline. The airline rule was that she could earn Frequent Flyer miles, but she couldn't use them on that route. Go figure! Okay—that was their rule, unreasonable as it seemed, so there was no basis for an argument on that issue. But, how could she use those miles?

Cory lived in Argentina for six months and Tracy wanted to visit him. Perfect timing to use the miles, right? Wrong! The dates of her trip didn't coordinate with the airline miles usage rules—rules that weren't written anywhere that we could easily see, but which made it difficult to argue. Yes, I know that there are usually blackout dates, but this didn't make sense for her travel dates—no high traffic time, etc. I tried to argue, but didn't put much into it, since I didn't have any real ammunition.

Next strategy—I suggested that she use her miles to upgrade to First Class for such a long trip. Airline wins again—they wouldn't let her use the miles. Another idea—if she gets to the airport, and finds that there are empty upgrade seats, she should try to use the miles at that point. How could they deny her that option, if the seats were available? Wrong again! They wouldn't let her use the miles, despite the empty seats. Ironically, when Cory traveled to Argentina on the same airline, they gave him a complimentary upgrade to First Class, since there were seats available. And, he didn't have to use miles—they simply offered. Nothing seemed to be logical with this airline. Tracy started to think that her brother was the Golden Child and if they could, the airline would probably have made her travel in Cargo.

I had found a reasonable and logical argument for her to use her Frequent Flyer miles. Tracy had been able to earn miles going back and forth to school. She had been prevented from using those miles on any of those trips based on some non-logical internal Corporate centered, customer unfriendly basis. She couldn't use them for the ticket to Argentina based on some other anti-customer internal Corporate protocol. Now, she wasn't able to upgrade when there was availability.

At this point, I tried to go up the ladder in the company. I went through a Customer Service supervisor, who couldn't give me any reason for the ongoing obstacles. It was pretty obvious that customer service wasn't high on the airline's list of priorities. So, I went through other channels to get to the Executive office. This was one of the worst stonewalls that I have ever experienced. I can usually at least get to the Administrative Assistants to a President, CEO, Vice President, or someone at a high level, and those assistants can often be very helpful. Instead, with this airline, I reached "I don't know who", since she wouldn't give me her title. My goal was to find a way for Tracy to use her miles, pointing out the unreasonable barriers she had experienced. When I pointed out how difficult it was to reach Executive, Ms. Anonymous said that the airline was getting too many calls so they eliminated staff to deal with the calls, preferring to respond to emails. What a wonderful way to say "We don't care". At that point, I gave up—for then.

About a year later, Tracy told me that she had received a message that her miles had expired. At this point, I was furious and hell-bent on confronting the fact that the airline was so customer unfriendly. I would definitely find a way to reinstate those miles. One day, I saw an article in the newspaper about ways in which airlines were customer unfriendly, especially related to their Frequent Flier programs. What a great opportunity for me to take action! I contacted the person who had written the article, and asked for his suggestions, though wondering if I could accomplish this goal so far down the pike. He was very helpful and gave me contact information for Executive areas within the airline. I emailed the President and two Vice Presidents, summarizing the issue and asking that they designate someone to get back to me to resolve the problem. Two of the emails came back "Access Denied". Not a standard "Undeliverable" email message, but "Access Denied"—another way of saying "We don't want to hear from you; we don't care". Here we go again—No, wait, I'm not giving up yet. I forwarded the email to the one person whose email was not blocked, and said:

"Please see the email below. I was attempting to resolve a Frequent Flier problem for my daughter, and at the suggestion of a travel reporter, wrote to you and two of your Vice Presidents. As you can see, delivery failed to the two Vice Presidents. I don't know if this is a technical issue, or, with the "Access Denied" message, this is your company's attempt to stonewall its customers. I would hope that it is the former, rather than the latter. I would appreciate your forwarding my issue to an appropriate person for resolution. I would love to be able to get back to the travel reporter to let him know that your company does, indeed, value their customers. That would certainly be a better topic for a future column than one which details continued stonewalling. Thank you."

In this email, I challenged the President to step up to the Customer Service plate and also held out the idea that if there is no response, there is a consequence—I could go back to the travel reporter with my negative outcome and this could possibly result in negative press.

The email challenge worked. I received a call from a representative, Ava, designated by someone in Executive. Her initial message was friendly and inviting. When I called, she was chipper and quick to say that Tracy's miles hadn't expired, and that she had used most of them on a vacation package two years earlier through their Travel subsidiary, but didn't go on the trip and didn't have the miles reinstated. I had forgotten about the cancelled trip. Now, I remembered. However, I was positive that Tracy had asked for reinstatement of miles, and confirmed this with her. The bad news was that she hadn't documented how she did that. *(Always remember to document the important detail in a situation like this one.)* While Tracy hadn't documented the reinstatement request, I was confident that she was correct that she had reinstated the miles, knowing that she wouldn't have simply allowed the airline to retain them, and I also remembered that when she cancelled the trip, she had told me that she had gotten everything back.

Ava lost her chipper tone when I argued that Tracy had taken care of the miles issue. She couldn't find any documentation. However, she did let slip that the problem in finding documentation was their system issue. They simply don't have access. And, she was choosing to pass the buck to their Travel Division. At that point, since I was in a Customer Service area designated by Executive, this area should be able to coordinate with their Travel section to address the issue. My goal was to have her coordinate with that area to reinstate the miles. At this point, she started to argue with me, and then said that since Tracy was over 21, she would have to deal with Tracy. This was fine with me. She volunteered to call Tracy the next day. When almost a week went by without a call, I went back to Executive, and sent this email:

"Please see copies of emails below, in which I describe a problem that my daughter had with your airline. The email was sent to a travel reporter. I have also added another email to him, summarizing last week's experience with your representative, Ava. Ava was to contact my daughter last Wednesday to address the issue. She failed to follow through. Added to the incredible difficulty in dealing with your airline as a whole, it appears that Ava was quick to respond when she believed that the issue only required a simple answer. Now, with the situation a bit more complicated, it has become clear that she (the airline?) is not interested in serving the customer. Certainly this is a logical conclusion based on her tone when I pointed out the problem. This is underscored by her failure to contact my daughter. If the airline is really interested in providing good customer service, I would think that the next step would be to have Ava's manager—some manager—contact me or my daughter. We are both available by telephone. I will hope for a timely contact, before I get back to the travel reporter. Thank you."

Once again, I was clear on the issue, and challenged the airline's management on commitment to customer service. Again, I held out the consequence of possible negative publicity. While my position that Tracy had requested reinstatement wasn't as firmly backed up as I would have liked, I did have a reasonable and logical position. The chain of events that underscored the airline's lack of customer service strengthened that position. When I didn't receive a response to the email in the next two days, I called one of the Vice

President numbers that had been given to me by the reporter. I reached the VP's Administrative Assistant, and explained the issue briefly, focusing on the lack of current responsiveness from the representative and the lack of response to the last email to the VP. Her demeanor said that she was someone who would have put up a wall, but I was insistent.

The next day, a supervisor in Executive called me. The supervisor informed me that they would be making an "Exception", since they don't generally reinstate miles so far down the road. While the supervisor was trying to be helpful, there is one problem with her thinking—this shouldn't be considered an "Exception". The word, "Exception" says "I'm doing you a favor". She wasn't doing me a favor. She was doing what was right, based on the pattern of poor customer service. I told her that I appreciated her efforts, and would certainly accept reinstatement of miles, but explained why "Exception" isn't a good word choice. She got it. This wasn't argument for argument's sake, but rather, in order to accomplish goals, it is important to try to change the thinking on the opposite end. If this person thinks that she is doing me a favor, she doesn't understand that providing good service to a customer is the critical standard of performance, and not a "favor". We had earned reinstatement because of our hassles with the airline.

While she could have talked about restrictions on use of miles—which she wisely didn't do—she did see that there was a problem. When we talked about "Exceptions", I also mentioned Ava's failure to get back to Tracy. Here, we had an interesting discussion. She said that she had spoken to Ava, who told her that she had tried to reach Tracy, but didn't leave a message. I jumped on this. Ava's statement was certainly an attempt to cover her tracks. If she had really tried to call, she would have left a message—she had left one for me on her initial call. The supervisor couldn't argue with this, and this small piece of information underlined my ongoing problem, weakening any potential argument that the supervisor may consider. And we did have one last little piece of business—

The last piece of the issue was the reinstatement fee. There was a fee of $150 to reinstate miles. I don't know what occurred when Tracy originally had them reinstated two years earlier—we don't have a record of having been charged a fee. However, fees often go up over time. This was especially true of the airlines after the spike in oil prices. Airlines had added all kinds of new fees and they increased old ones. It wasn't logical to believe that this airline hadn't increased their fees over the two years since the loss of miles. Based on this logic, I told her that I believed that we should pay the same fee that was in place two years ago. When I posed this issue to the supervisor, she said that she didn't think that there had been an increase over the last two years. I would have been okay with that if she could prove it.

I asked her to review her records, to find the fee for reinstatement of miles two years ago. As with the mile loss, there was no company documentation. Armed with this information and my logic regarding increasing fees, I asked for a reduced reinstatement fee. She wasn't happy about this, and said that they never adjust the fee. I pointed out that, based on the strong probability that there had been a fee increase, most likely within the past year, the incredibly poor customer service up to this time, and my time spent in resolving a problem that shouldn't have become this overblown to begin with, it wasn't unreasonable to reduce the fee. Worn out, and not having an argument to my logic, she finally agreed.

Tracy got her miles back. I made a point. Will that point have any impact in the company? I'm not so sure that it will in a company that has created so many barriers to obtaining good customer service. However, *it is always a good idea to make the points, because, once again, if nobody hears, nothing changes. And, I made sure to document all of the detail—supervisor name, contact information for her and for the Executive area, and the agreed upon resolution, to make sure that if there is a snafu, I have documentation. And, in case there is a next time.*

WE COUNT—YOU DON'T

There are Corporate policies/charges where the consumer perspective is totally lost. A few examples:

Howard and I were planning a trip and decided to use Frequent Flier miles. Neither of us had enough miles for a free ticket in our individual accounts, but by transferring miles from one account to the other, we would have enough for one ticket. When Howard transferred miles from his account to mine, we were charged over $200 just for the miles transfer.

What service was rendered that warranted a charge? None. I did a little checking and found that most airlines charge a fee for miles transfer and that there is not any substantive service that is covered by this charge. While I understand that the airlines have had to add charges in order to be profitable, and I don't like most of those charges, they at least represent something tangible. There is no reason for a charge to transfer miles other than "Because we can."

Many hotels charge for WiFi access. This is a disingenuous charge because it doesn't cost the hotel to offer WiFi to guests; if WiFi is available, it's available—period. But, it can be a moneymaker, especially when some hotels charge as much as $20 or more per day for access. I have gone to hotel managers or to Executive offices to arrange waiver of the WiFi charge. I have never had anyone say no—they have always waived the charge. But, what is the reason for the charge? "Because we can."

Cory and Tracy have travelled frequently by train. They found that the railroad reduces the fare by 10% with certain association membership discounts. However, if the booking is made less than three days prior to travel or if there is a change in schedule within that three day window, the discount doesn't apply.

I called the railroad's Media Relations Department and asked the reason for the three day window policy. The representative explained that a higher charge for a booking closer to the travel date was standard in all travel services—hotels, airlines, and railroad. This may be the case, but I've seen a wide range of prices close to travel dates versus earlier booking dates. Sometimes they're the same, sometimes higher and sometimes lower. So, why the discount limitation? "Because we can."

I haven't managed to change these consumer unfriendly policies. But, there's still time. *"Because we can" is never a good reason for anything.*

RELATIONSHIPS—THEY LOVE ME/THEY LOVE ME NOT

IF YOU WON'T TAKE MY CALLS, I'LL FIND YOU ANYWAY

Pharmacy Benefit Managers (PBMs) are companies that contract with medical insurance companies or with employers to manage healthcare prescription benefits. In my role as a health advocate, I was helping Mr. Smith, who had a prescription coverage problem when he changed jobs and fell through the PBM cracks.

Mr. Smith had worked for an employer that contracted with a PBM to administer his prescription benefit. When he changed jobs, he found that his new employer used the same PBM as his old employer. He refilled a prescription just after the job change. Unknown to Mr. Smith, the prescription was accidentally filled through the old employer's drug benefit. Many months later, he received a dunning notice, saying that he owed the PBM $240 for the prescription.

Although Mr. Smith had never seen the $240 because he simply used what he thought was the correct coverage to fill the prescription, the PBM went after him with a vengeance, to the point where they were threatening to send him to Collections. It seemed that this could have had an easy solution—call the PBM, ask them to back out the payment from the old company and transfer the charge to the funding for the new company. Same PBM, two different employers—no problem, right? Wrong.

I started by calling the PBM Customer Service Department on Mr. Smith's behalf. The representative said that they couldn't correct the problem. I asked for a supervisor, who said the same thing. Frequently, employer groups have Account Managers within the PBMs and insurers, who work on issues related to the specific employers. I located the Account Managers for both employers. Same story—neither could get the problem corrected. Why was I having a problem? This was the same PBM for both employers, two different "pots". Just transfer from one "pot" to the other. Simple. Logical. But complex within the PBM bureaucracy.

Having attempted to go through normal channels, it was now time to go up the ladder. I Googled the PBM's Corporate Headquarters and found the name and phone number of their CEO. I didn't need to speak to the CEO, himself. I just needed someone in that Executive area who had some clout over multiple areas and could make the right thing happen. I had the misfortune to deal with the CEO's assistant, June. She referred me to an Operations Manager to try to fix the problem. The Operations Manager really tried, but he couldn't get it right, either.

There was no way that I was going to walk away without fixing the problem. I called June back—many times. I spoke with her a few times and always got some type of Corporate Speak from her, but no action. Since there was nowhere else to go other than directly to the CEO himself (and I'd have to go through her to get to him), I decided that advocacy through pestering would be my only option—along with the promise that if the situation didn't get fixed, I could suggest that Mr. Smith may want to go to the media. A great human interest/broken healthcare system story—big company versus little "Everyman" news article. *Remember, I don't threaten—I promise*, and I would definitely have done that if I had to.

RELATIONSHIPS—THEY LOVE ME/THEY LOVE ME NOT

I finally got to a point where I had left numerous messages, and hadn't heard back from June. I knew that either she wasn't returning my messages, or, when she saw my Caller ID, she would let the phone go to voice mail. *It was time to get creative.*

Instead of calling June's direct number, I called the general Corporate number. This number allowed me to select an option from a list of employees. I had the name of the CEO, and I hit the prompt for his name. June could avoid my calls when I dialed her number, but she was forced to pick up when the phone rang on her boss's line. I had her!

When she picked up, I calmly, but edgily, pointed out that I had left at least five messages for her, with no return calls. She told me that she had been busy. I explained that I am sympathetic to "busy", and that I am busy as well, but that I am well aware that she was avoiding my calls. At that point, what the hell—"I know that you're sick of me", I said, "and I'm not too thrilled with you either. But I'm going to make this situation right." I told her that I would do whatever it took to make that happen—if it meant going to the media, speaking with her boss or I could come up with other creative ideas to resolve the problem. She heard me. She finally got the problem fixed. I don't know how she did it and why it couldn't be done much earlier other than Corporate Think/ Corporate Speak, the fact that she simply didn't care or that she was just lazy. Whatever the reason, the process had been unacceptable.

The point here is that I used all logical, simple, reasonable options to fix the problem, starting through normal channels and going through all of the options that I could think of to solve the problem. Tenacity was a big part of the resolution. I pretty much became "The Thing That Wouldn't Die". Getting creative by playing with the phone triage system was the final blow. I was stuck dealing with someone who didn't care and who didn't think that I could penetrate her fortress. She was greatly mistaken. Was it mean spirited to put the cards on the table and tell her that I knew that she didn't like me and that I didn't care for her either? Yeah, pretty much. But being clear and blunt, I showed her that there was nothing that she could do to continue to put obstacles in my way. Like a science fiction monster, I would penetrate any obstacle she could put in my path—Corporate Speak, excuses—nothing would deter me. I would achieve my goal—if not pleasantly, then taking her lead, with any strategy that would get beyond her stonewalling. It worked.

My preference and general style is to create positive relationships with contacts. Most of the time it works, but once in a while it doesn't. June didn't become my BFF, but I can live with that.

WINDOWS OF TIME AND HOW TO CLOSE THEM

Working on a healthcare advocacy case, I was trying to arrange an Appeals hearing for a client with an insurer who would only give a four hour time frame on the one day a week that they held hearings. This is not the norm in this type of situation—scheduling Appeals hearings is generally more consumer friendly. But this insurer could pretty much have been a cable company or delivery service. I've had better dealings with furniture delivery schedules than I did with this insurer's scheduling protocol.

Patients have legal rights to be able to present their arguments when a service has been denied—usually in a written argument, but for this situation, in a hearing. In this case, it was essential for the doctor to be on the call. The doctor had patients all day on the hearing date. But, she had a one hour window, from 1 PM to 2 PM, when she could get on the phone for five minutes. Five minutes was all that we needed.

The Appeals hearing coordinator, Janet, gave me the bureaucratese, "We only have hearings on Thursdays, and we have a lot of cases, so we don't know what time, blah, blah, blah....". "That's fine," I said, "but she's entitled to a hearing with whatever support she needs to make her argument. So, I understand if you can't think out of the box. I'll call the Appeals Manager, and we'll make it happen." And that's just what I did. Janet called me back (grudgingly) after my call to the manager.

"I can do it between 12:30 and 1:30." (Remember, doctor's office said 1 PM to 2 PM.) I called the doctor's office to see if this would work—it wouldn't. Having laid the groundwork, Janet and the doctor's office needed to duke out the detail. "If you can't make it happen on Thursday" I said, "you will need to work out a different day, with a specially convened committee, so that the patient can have her opportunity to appeal. You need to call the doctor's office." She called me back and said that they would hear the patient's case at 1 PM.

As with June at the PBM, I would have preferred a simple and friendly solution in this situation. So, Janet isn't my BFF either. And, once again, I can live with that.

DON'T BE TAKEN FOR GRANTED

Building relationships is usually an asset in accomplishing your goals, and long-term loyalties can yield good outcomes. However, loyalties can turn into being taken for granted if you're not careful. Take a look at the car dealership problems.

Howard and I tend to stay with car manufacturers and dealerships for long periods of time, which creates relationships with Sales and Service staff. However, our relationship with one dealership took many interesting twists and turns and didn't end well—for them. How many problems did we have? Many. But, they were always resolvable—until they weren't.

The windshield and the wind deflector would solidify my place in the "I hate this customer/I give up/She wins" journey that would seal my legacy with this dealer. It wasn't my goal to be the least popular customer at this dealership. But, you do what you have to do.

On a very hot day, Howard and I took a long ride. The air conditioner was on in the car. We drove on the highway and parked in an open field parking lot. We were in a museum for about an hour. When we came out, there was a long crack in the windshield. Having driven on the highway with no problems, and being in an open field where there was nothing around to cause the crack, the logical conclusion was that the crack was caused by the combination of extreme heat and air conditioning. In other words, this was a glass defect. I took the car in to have the windshield replaced —under the warranty. Jeff, the manager of the Service area, looked at the windshield, and said: "A stone hit it."

I replied: "There was no stone, there is not a spot which shows the beginning of the crack where a stone would have hit, and we were not in a situation where there would have been a stone around to hit it. No stones on the highway, nothing but air above us on the parking lot." Jeff argued. I argued. "Turn it in to your insurance", he said. I replied, "This is a warranty issue". I persisted. He replaced the windshield. *The moral of this story is that you have to have a clear case and you have to be prepared to stand your ground.*

Windshield fixed. And then, the wind deflector. What is a wind deflector? It was a plastic panel under the front end of the car, designed to protect the car from wind. Why? I don't know. Did we ever know it was there? No. Until it broke. We were driving on the New Jersey Turnpike and started to hear a strange sound—like metal dragging. We pulled over. Howard looked under the front of the car. He saw a large piece of plastic hanging down from the underside of the front end. He wedged himself partway under the car, scuffed his jacket, but managed to get the deflector pushed back up so that we could drive.

When we took the car to the dealership, Jeff said that we must have hit something. We didn't hit something—this was a design flaw. (The manufacturer later eliminated this design piece, underscoring my point.) The design flaw caused a problem—a dangerous one, where we were on the side of a busy road, trying to make the car driveable. The piece needed to be replaced and stabilized—under warranty. Jeff tried to stand his ground. I spoke with Greg, our salesman, thinking that our loyalty meant something and he should get involved if he

RELATIONSHIPS—THEY LOVE ME/THEY LOVE ME NOT

wanted to keep a customer. I spoke with Bob, the owner of the dealership. Greg was too mild mannered, and didn't do much. Bob was rude. I was angry.

Back to my Corporate contact from my gas gauge issue. When I called my VP, I found that Jeff had already contacted the manufacturer's Corporate office. He told them that the wind deflector was hit by a stone! The same stone that hit the windshield a year earlier, I guess! I was furious. Jeff forgot who he was dealing with. My Vice President called the dealership and told them to fix it under warranty. But, that wasn't enough for me. The whole incident was more aggravating than it needed to be. I needed an apology in order to make the dealership understand how badly they had violated our trust and long relationship. My Vice President spoke with Bob and Jeff, and I received apologies from both of them.

The point of these stories is that, although we were long-standing customers, having bought six cars from them over several years—a lot of cars and a lot of years—that didn't seem to make a difference. With our long relationship, it was logical and appropriate for me to talk to Greg and Jeff about supporting my reasonable requests. I expected them to resolve the problems quickly and with minimal aggravation—based on both the relationship and the desire to keep a customer. That's a good assumption in some cases, but not in this case. I found that Greg was a wuss, and Bob was too full of himself to be customer oriented, forgetting that his agenda should be "I need/want to keep this customer". So I went the other route—above them to Corporate, which resolved the issue.

As a bonus, Jeff and I became BFF. He gave up, worn out, knowing that I'd find a way to accomplish my goals. I think that his final conclusion was "Why fight anymore?" And we lived happily ever after until we moved on to another car dealership. The change in dealers came when Greg took our longstanding relationship for granted when we decided to trade in our car.

We had been driving about a year prior to trade in, and were rear ended by an SUV. Our car was repaired and we had no problems. Since the car had been hit when we were out of the area, it was fixed there. Because we weren't so confident in the out of area dealership, we spoke with our own dealership to make sure that the out of area dealer was repairing the car properly. Jeff was kind enough to handle the coordination on the repair.

When we decided to trade in the car, Greg, aware of the accident, worked the numbers with an appraisal on the car that would require that we pay $1000 to trade the car in. A negative value for trade in! I pointed out the fact that there was no defect in the car despite the accident, the value of the car wasn't a negative $1000, and reminded him of our longstanding relationship.

He went back to the drawing board, and came back with what he described as "exciting" news. He had worked the numbers so that it would be an even trade. So, we wouldn't owe $1000; we would break even. I won't repeat what I said to him; my mother would have said that it wasn't ladylike. Aside from my unprintable comments, I told him that there were other dealerships. He didn't get it. And, I don't think that it occurred to him that we would leave after all of those cars and all of those years. We did go to another dealership. They offered us $4000 in trade.

I never called Greg back. He called to follow up. When I told him that we had bought from another dealership, he was truly floored. So, while loyalty can be a good thing, and relationships can work for you, be wary of the players, what they understand and don't understand, and their agendas. This all adds up to how and if loyalties and relationships affect the bottom line. In our situation with this dealership, we were taken for granted rather than being treated as loyal and valued customers.

It's best to remember to be wary and that, loyalty or not, no one can corner or defeat you unless you let it happen.

WITH STRINGS ATTACHED: PERKS- HOW TO MAKE THE MOST OF THEM

REBATE CARDS—FIGURING OUT THE PUZZLE

There is a yin/yang to Rebate cards. Large corporations often use them as promotional incentives to make it appear that you are receiving a discount on a purchase. A Rebate card can be a nice perk. But you have to figure out all of the ins and outs in order to get the rebated discount.

What is wrong with Rebate cards? They're disingenuous. You purchase an item for an advertised special price. For example, an item (cell phone, appliance, etc.) may be advertised at $99. If you read the small print, you will often find "after rebate". Unless you make sure to go after the rebate, you are paying a higher price than what was advertised. And it is a struggle to get that differential between the list price and the "discounted" price. You have to cut the UPC code off of the box. Not easy—cutting cardboard isn't like cutting through butter. You have to fill out the form and make sure that you copy the serial number correctly—no mistakes. You need a copy of the sales receipt. You get everything together, and make a copy for your records. Get it into the envelope, put a stamp on it, and mail it. That's not a discount; that's work! Most companies now have an online option for registering rebates. It's still too much work.

A few warnings—It can take six to eight weeks to receive the Rebate card. Make sure that you remember to look for it—if it doesn't arrive, call the company that sold the rebate eligible item. Better yet, keep a copy of the form, which should have a phone number for the Rebate department. Look for the card expiration date. While many people think that Federal law regulating Gift cards applies to Rebate cards, this is not the case. A Rebate card is not a Gift card. Gift cards have a minimum expiration of five years. Rebate cards do not. My Rebate card for a cell phone purchase arrived at the end of January and had an expiration date of May. It's more like buying groceries than having a Gift card—shelf life is limited.

It costs money for companies to issue Rebate cards. They have processing costs, mailing costs, staff costs. So, why would they set up a system that costs them to maintain it? Because in the end, the savings from unused Rebate cards outweighs the cost of setting up the Rebate system. Businesses know that many Rebate cards are never used. Many people don't bother to send in the forms. Customers don't always keep track, and may not realize that the card never arrived. If the form or online detail is lost, you either have to track down the information through the store or the manufacturer (if you're lucky enough to locate someone to help you to find it) or you're screwed. Believing that the Rebate card can't expire quickly, many people ignore the expiration date. Think of all of those unclaimed rebates! Corporations do—in fact, many count on it.

Okay. Now you have the card. But using it can be a challenge. I have found that hotels frequently won't take them. If you use them in a restaurant, even if you leave a cash tip, there is often a "hold" on a percentage for the tip, with the funds released later, causing confusion because you have to know the balance on the card in order to avoid having it rejected for insufficient funds.

The card says "Debit", but must be coded by the merchant as a "Credit" card. On my card, the activation sticker said: "This is not a credit card"—more confusion. If the amount of the charge is more than the amount of the Rebate card, the merchant has to run the Rebate card for the balance amount on the card before running the other method of payment. Ultimately, all of this confusion can result in embarrassment if the card is declined—which happens frequently.

Of course, I experienced a decline on my cell phone Rebate card. Howard and I were making a purchase and knew that the cost was more than the Rebate card, so we gave the cashier a credit card as well. She ran them in different ways—Rebate card first, then credit card first, as a credit transaction, as a debit transaction—nothing worked. We gave up and paid with a credit card. When we got home, I contacted the Customer Service number on the card. The representative could see the attempted transaction but couldn't tell me why it didn't go through. She told me that she'd had many similar complaints and that she was trying to work with a supervisor to figure out how to use the card so that it wouldn't reject. Obviously, I wasn't the only person having a problem.

Remember my escalated contact—my new BFF—from the cell phone problems? Since this rebate problem wasn't resolving through standard channels and was related to the cell phone purchase, I went back to that escalated contact. She went to the Marketing Department, home of the Rebate promotion. We discussed that I would try it once more, but she was poised to escalate if necessary.

I was finally able to use the card in a supermarket. The swipe pad asked for type of payment that included a category option labeled "Debit/Credit". Did that make it go through? I don't know. Interestingly, a few weeks later, we had lunch with a friend who used a Rebate card to try to pay the bill. Her card rejected, too, despite having checked a balance before she used it. She also finally used it in a supermarket—coincidence? Who knows?

What did I do to make the card work?

1. I followed all of the instructions for obtaining the card and kept records in case it never arrived.

2. I questioned through normal channels when it didn't work.

3. I escalated through my old contact within the company that was offering the Rebate card so that my problem would be addressed and also so that it could be reviewed on a broader level.

4. Although my contact was helpful, for this issue, she was an intermediary. I wanted the problem fixed for me, but I also wanted to be heard on a Corporate

level for all consumers. For that reason, I asked for the appropriate person above her who had a relationship with Marketing, the department in the company with jurisdiction over Rebate cards. When I spoke to this last person, I explained my view of the squirrely nature of Rebate cards and offered the polite challenge that her company could be the first to be the Good Guys by just discounting the phone, as opposed to playing games with the rebate. She couldn't make it happen, but could take the issue back to the people in charge.

Finally, I received a response from the Rebate team through this last contact. It was really long. In a nutshell, it was a bit defensive and didn't address the problem. It contained information that I already knew—like the fact that Debit is printed on the front of the card, as is the expiration date, the customer is responsible for knowing the balance on the card—and on and on. Since I knew all of this and it didn't answer the question, this wasn't a useful response. But I especially liked the part that said that the customer can access the balance by going to the website, texting for the balance or calling the Customer Service number. That isn't always convenient when you're in the middle of a transaction. Not to mention that you can know the balance but still experience a rejection—as in the problem scenarios that I've mentioned already.

The company response was very earnest. The operant word here is "earnest"—from a narrow perspective that was coming from someone who lived in "Corporate World" and was earnestly trying to present the Corporate party line. In other words, it was "Corporate Speak"—an explanation that is disconnected from the real world where consumers live.

Ultimately, I'm not so sure that Rebate cards are going to disappear; the marketing strategy and advantage to the corporations are too strong. But, there have been lawsuits filed on this issue based on confusion and restrictions.

What can you do? Make sure that you follow all of the instructions so that you receive and use the card. If you have a problem, make noise. Making noise should resolve your specific problem. And, if more cards are redeemed and if enough voices are heard, maybe the system will change.

PROMOTION OR CONFUSION—GETTING THE BEST PRICE

Most retailers have special sales to entice their customers to buy. Finding the optimal time to obtain the best price can be quite a challenge. There is a department store that often has One Day sales. That sounds special, but when it seems to happen every week or every few weeks, it gets a little old. But it really can be a money saver if you look for the special prices during these sales. Of course, these sales are often followed by other promotions so that it becomes sort of like gaming the stock market—you just can't accurately predict the peak timing for best outcome. This store is not alone. Almost all retailers have their own version of special promotions. That's a good thing—it's just that figuring them out can sometimes be confusing.

Look at my adventures in the "get the best deal" game. Like many other retailers, one of my favorites allows their cardholders to earn rewards for spending and also sends out special offers. The rewards are used as cash towards a purchase. Special offers include Make Your Own Sale day, which gives the customer a percentage off of a total purchase. There are a number of other offers that come my way during the year. While I appreciate these perks, most of these special offers and rewards have disclaimers on the back, some of which are clear, and some of which aren't. Clear ones include the fact that they are not valid with employee discounts or at outlet stores. Unclear ones include language that says that they are not valid with other promotions. The problem arises when you try to define promotion.

According to Merriam-Webster's Collegiate Dictionary, a promotion is defined as *"the furtherance of the acceptance and sale of merchandise through advertising, publicity or discounting"*. In the real world of retail, I haven't a clue as to what this really means. In my world, I just want to get the best price through legitimate means without a hassle.

During a pre-Christmas rush of special offers, I went into the store. They had a Buy One Get One sweater sale (promotion?). I had a special offer coupon for 30% off of a total purchase, valid during a specific three day period. The problem with this offer was that it was valid during the same time period as the Buy One Get One sale. There were so many promotions at the same time that it was virtually impossible to use the 30% coupon. Was the Buy One Get One a promotion so that the 30% coupon couldn't be used with that offer? I guess so, since the reward wouldn't scan. I was okay with this—the coupon wouldn't go through the computer system other than to void the Buy One Get One, so that, in essence, the customer had a choice of price—with the coupon or with the offer. I guess that's fair.

However, beware of computer systems. They don't always scan accurately, making the situation more confusing. If the final price doesn't look right, have Sales or Management staff check it. If the system is wrong, they can generally do a manual override.

The customer unfriendly problem in this scenario was that the 30% coupon felt like a manipulation—it was a way to lure the customer into the store, but with minimal opportunity to use the coupon.

Another store policy and system problem occurred when Tracy bought a jacket in her local branch of the store. I had a $20 reward at home and wanted to use it, but she didn't have it at the time of purchase. So, the logical and simple thought was that she could give me the receipt, I could go to the local branch, present the reward, have them credit her purchase, and re-do the purchase with the reward. Simple? Not really.

I went to the local store within about a week or two of her purchase. Remember, I'm not returning the jacket; I simply wanted to use a reward that had been available at the time of purchase but wasn't used because Tracy was in one city while I had the reward in another city at the time of the original purchase. When the cashier tried to adjust the purchase, the sale price had been discontinued, and he had difficulty getting the same price into the computer. This didn't make sense. How was this different than if I were exchanging one item for another if it was defective or the wrong size? In those cases, I should have the same price, since I was purchasing the same item. My situation was analogous—I was returning an item and buying the same item. Customer service wasn't a problem. The computer system was the problem. This cashier was customer service oriented and savvy. He found a way to get the sale price and the reward through the system. But it shouldn't have been so complicated.

To complicate matters further, I had received a 15% Make Your Own Sale Day coupon. I went into the store with Tracy on a day when the store was offering an additional 30% off on Sale items. When I went to the register, I was told that the 15% wasn't valid with the 30% off Sale. I asked the cashier to scan the 15% offer, and if it didn't scan, I would go with that, and consider it invalid. But, it did scan. Nice deal!

The next time I went to this store, they had a 40% off one regular priced item offer. A coupon wasn't required on that particular day. I had a $20 reward. Remember, a reward is not a coupon. It is something that is earned for having spent with the company. The Merriam-Webster Collegiate Dictionary defines reward as *"a stimulus administered to an organism following a correct or desired response that increases the probability of occurrence of the response"* or *"something that is given in return for good or evil done or received or that is offered or given for some service or attainment"*. While the language is a bit lofty, it is clear that the reward is earned and the goal is to "increase the desired response" (more shopping—good or evil, depending on your point of view).

I went to the cashier with my sweater, presented my reward, and was unceremoniously told that the reward couldn't be used on the 40% off item. Once again, I asked the clerk to scan the reward, and if it scanned, fine, and if not, I'll hold onto the reward. This clerk was not so customer oriented, and refused to scan the reward. Here we go—I asked for the manager. A hissy manager came over and initially refused to scan the reward. I insisted. Insistence (politely but firmly—or edgily—whatever it takes, but start nicely) was a powerful tool. It was clear that I wasn't going anywhere, so he scanned the reward. It scanned. He allowed the scan to go through, but his attitude was testy, and his pounding on the computer keys certainly wasn't customer friendly. To avoid future problems in this store with this edgy manager, I asked for his name and the name and phone number of the Regional Manager. He gave me the name of the Regional Manager, but with the standard Customer Service toll free line. I tried to obtain a direct line to the Regional Manager, but he wouldn't give it to me. I promised (as usual, I promised, not threatened) to locate her to address the issue.

When I called the toll free number, I found that I had been given the Online Customer Service number. After about ten minutes of pounding the keys for different prompts, I finally reached a representative. (Take note—harder key pounding and spouting "F-This" doesn't connect you to a live representative.)

PERKS - WITH STRINGS ATTACHED

I finally reached a representative. I was told that they needed to transfer me to Guest Services. So far that day, I hadn't felt like a Guest. I reached someone who tried to talk about policy. When I told him that I was simply interested in speaking with the Regional Manager, he responded that the Regional Manager doesn't speak with customers. Here was his way of saying "Customers don't count". This is unacceptable—and, as I later found out, untrue. The Regional Manager has direct responsibility for store operations. Interaction with customers is critical to being able to do the job effectively to meet store and consumer needs. Also, although many companies have policies that insulate certain staff from their consumer base, remember that *no company employee is above dealing with the consumers who ultimately pay their salary.*

I wasn't interested in hearing policy from a first line representative. I needed to talk to the person who would have impact in the store and with the Corporate level—the Regional Manager. I finally reached a supervisor. When I explained the reward/Make Your Own Sale Day issue, he asked me if I had read the legal language on the back of the reward. Interesting, but a bit dim-witted. While the company has the right to list their conditions, those conditions should be clear rather than ambiguous. Not to mention that they should be simple, since customers shouldn't have to bring a lawyer to the store when they want to use a reward or special offer. He also said that the protocol for sending callers through their National line was to triage the calls to the appropriate area, and he would do that and also send me a promotion as compensation for my time.

I received a call back from the Regional Manager. She was responsive to my issues and was in a position to have impact. I felt that she heard and understood the problem. And, the supervisor in Guest Services did send me a $40 reward, the promised promotion. So, the reward underscores the dictionary definition so that their administration of a "stimulus" got the desired result—it got me back into the store. The reward was a nice perk and the discussion with the Regional Manager made me feel that my interaction had impact, and hopefully, would have an effect on company operations.

Whether it was my adventure or other factors, this chain has become more customer friendly. I can see customer service focus, and I have continued to shop there, happy with the service.

CUSTOMER SERVICE—THE INS AND OUTS

PUTTING HOSPITABLE BACK INTO THE HOSPITALITY INDUSTRY (THE COUPLE WHO GROWS TOGETHER ADVOCATES TOGETHER)

Howard and I are close to our 40th wedding anniversary. No, I am not as old as the Gloria Stuart character in "Titanic". We just married Shakespearean style—we were 14 when we got married—or so it seems.

Some people say that when two people are a couple for a long time they start to look alike. Some also say that people start to look like their dogs. I'm not sure if the same people are saying both, but I don't believe either. I do, however, believe that a husband and wife can grow together. Howard and I have picked up on each other's skills and habits. Specifically, Howard has learned the ins and outs of being an effective consumer. And he has taught me to be more charming. We used this duality to address customer service problems on a weekend getaway.

We were going to a wedding in Boston and made it a getaway weekend by staying in New York first. Problem One happened as we left the hotel in New York. We stayed at a hotel where we are frequent guests and where getting in and out is easy. The garage is next door, and it usually takes less than ten minutes to get our car. Not this time. New garage management wasn't efficient. There was only one attendant who was letting a line of cars in while we were waiting to get out. What could we do? After about twenty minutes, Howard used his charm and assertiveness to coax a desk clerk onto the street to stop the cars coming in while another desk clerk called the garage attendant on the phone to let him in on the plan. It still took 45 minutes to get out but it would have taken longer if Howard hadn't spoken up.

I felt that we should be compensated for our inconvenience. I asked one of the desk clerks if the parking charge could be written off because of the problem. While he understood my point, he replied that the two businesses are separate. I told him that I understand this, but because of the relationship between the two, they should be able to work together to satisfy the guest. He said that he would try. When we got home, there was a message from the hotel saying that they were writing off the parking charge. *A point to remember—often, two separate businesses that work together can work together to your benefit, especially if they understand the need for good customer service to retain clientele.* Problem One solved with great customer service.

Problem Two occurred at the hotel in Boston. We reached the hotel around 2 PM. The Front Desk told us that the room would be ready by 3 PM. Around 3:30, we returned to dress for the wedding. Although the hotel had many wedding guests staying there and knew that the bus for the wedding ceremony was leaving at 5 PM, they told us that our room wasn't ready. Once again, Howard used his assertiveness and charm to let them know that this wasn't acceptable and that they needed to get us into a room right away so that we could dress for the wedding. The desk staff grudgingly hovered over the computer and found a room. Howard's insistence resolved this issue. If

CUSTOMER SERVICE—THE INS AND OUTS

he had simply taken "room not yet available" at face value, we never would have been ready for the wedding in time. *When you see that someone doesn't want to solve a problem that requires a quick solution, stand there and insist until you have a proper resolution.* This works most of the time—especially in hotels. (We've had too many experiences where we were told that our room wasn't ready at the designated check in time, but with firm insistence and a refusal to accept this answer, the staff invariably finds a room that is ready—usually an upgrade.)

Problem Three—We thought that the weekend was over until we received our credit card bill. I noticed that instead of a charge for one room, there were two room charges. *Always check your credit card bills; if you don't check, you may be paying a charge that's not legitimately yours.* Thinking that this was a simple error, Howard called our credit card company, who conferenced to the hotel. The hotel rep told us that this wasn't an erroneous extra room charge, but rather, a charge for cleaning the room because we were smoking. SMOKING! We are not smokers; we even had a non-smoking room request on our booking. Howard flipped out. I didn't blame him, especially since he was dealing with a young know- it-all who didn't understand customer service. That discussion ended with the credit card company putting the charge in dispute.

I was fuming! (But not smoking) Now it was my turn to take action. I called back and asked for the manager. The person who had spoken with Howard said that she was the manager. I later found that in this boutique hotel in the evening, they designate front desk staff as evening managers. This one knew how to be obnoxious with a smile in her voice, but didn't know much more. She told me that there was "evidentiary proof" that we had been smoking. This proof was apparently a photograph of ashes on the windowsill. I suggested that she test for DNA, since we don't smoke, which meant that staff or another guest would have been the guilty party. Realizing that

183

I was going nowhere, I emailed the Guest Services Manager and spoke to her and to the General Manager in the morning. They still didn't get it—not only was it offensive to accuse us of something we didn't do, placing a silent charge without any discussion was unacceptable and flagrantly anti-customer service. However, my firm insistence and Howard's putting the charge in dispute pushed them to remove the charge. I also asked for a $100 courtesy credit for our time and aggravation. The manager balked initially. But she caved when I told her that without a goodwill gesture, her skills in the service industry didn't amount to much.

Our yin/yang still works. Over the years, we've picked up on each other's strengths to work together when there is a problem—small or large. There are many keys to a good marriage. The most important one in our marriage is that we're lucky to have found our perfect mates. And, together, we can solve almost anything that comes our way.

DON'T SPEAK IN BUREAUCRATESE AND DON'T CALL ME MA'AM

To protect your credit cards, it's a good idea to register them with some form of registry that will provide security and the ability to act on your behalf if your cards are stolen. If you've ever had a card stolen, you know what I mean.

When Cory was an exchange student, he had his wallet stolen in Amsterdam. I'm not sure whether the moral of the story is not to let your child study abroad, not to let them have credit cards, or to make sure that they know not to hold on to a hanging strap on a crowded bus without using their free hand to hold onto the wallet in their pocket. The bottom line was that dealing with the stolen card was a problem, but the registry took care of it. However, if you're not receiving good customer service, dealing with the card registry can be a nuisance.

I had added a new card to our registry, and found that instead of adding me, they added Tracy—with her name spelled wrong. When I called to fix it, this should have been a simple call because I had added the card, and I was the user. I got about six words out of my mouth when the representative told me that she needed authorization from Howard to talk to me, since he is the prime account holder. Sometimes this happens when a couple shares a joint account, but not always. But

Howard wasn't available and in this case, this was bull from a bureaucrat. If she had listened and looked, she would have realized that I was correcting their error on an account with my name on it. (I learned in kindergarten that you should always listen and look when you are crossing the street. This applies to everything—I guess that she didn't go to the same kindergarten.)

Don't waste your time talking to a bureaucrat. Get the supervisor on the line. I did that. Unfortunately, the supervisor also got caught up in the bureaucratic "I need to speak to your husband" thing, and she, too, failed to listen. "Ma'am", she said, "I need to speak with the cardholder." (*NOTE*—If a US serviceman calls you Ma'am or Sir, this is a sign of respect—I learned this from watching *NCIS*. On the other hand, if you are in a conflict situation, and someone calls you Ma'am, they're really calling you "Bitch". I'm not sure of the comparable term for Sir, but I'm sure that there is one.) I disarmed her by saying "My name isn't Ma'am; it's Mauree Miller".

How do you resolve a situation like this and end what should have been a quick call that was going nowhere for way too long? I had documented the fact that on October 8, I spoke with representative Betty and added the new card. Since I, not Howard, had added the card, she should be able to pull the call that supported my position and then call me back to fix the problem. When she called back after she listened to the call recording, she said that yes, I was right, and she would fix the error. At that point, I got her to see that she and the first representative should have listened, and that we could have dealt with this much faster if they weren't so quick to quote bureaucratese rather than listen to the issue. Problem solved, and the supervisor and I became pretty much BFF. She got the point and would make it a staff training issue.

Call documentation is important. Because I had the call detail—when I called and the name of the representative—the supervisor found the detail necessary to solve the problem.

THESE BOOTS ARE MADE FOR SHOPPING

Tracy really wanted boots for her birthday. As a graduate student, with no income and much studying to do, my goal was to keep her in the library and out of department stores. But, sometimes, I was forced to deviate from that goal.

Just before Thanksgiving one year, one store had a "Friends and Family" 20% discount. So, I broke down and told Tracy that she could have the boots. She went to the store and found that they didn't have her size. But, she could order online. So, she ordered her boots online. I checked the online pricing when the boots arrived, and found that there was now a 30% discount online. (In store and online prices can sometimes differ.) Although this was only 10% differential, it was better in my pocket. But I decided to see what was happening in the store, because on Black Friday, with sales galore, I thought that there might be a further reduction. Sure enough, they were marked down to $199—a savings of $52 over the Friends and Family price.

Armed with the fact that they had been purchased only ten days earlier, I called the store's online number. (The boots had arrived only seven days earlier, since they had been shipped, which made it only a week from arrival to new sale price.) I told the representative about the in store sale.

CUSTOMER SERVICE—THE INS AND OUTS

The representative was accommodating, and called the store, but was told that the boots weren't on sale. Why had the store told me that they were on sale? While I thought that the representative had been given misinformation, I decided to drop the store issue, and just asked her to match the 30% discount. She tried to work with me, but as she attempted to put the discount in the system, she found that it wouldn't go through because, with the ten day window from time of order (not time of receipt), the transaction was closed (which meant that she couldn't get back into the system on this charge). This whole interaction had taken too long. At that point, I thanked her for trying to be helpful, and asked for a manager.

The manager got on the phone, and tried to be helpful. I explained the situation. It was reasonable to make the adjustment, and while she was at it, either the representative or I had been given misinformation, so I asked her to call the store again, to determine whether there was a greater reduction. She agreed, and called the store. The call to the store dropped, and I landed on Hold again. But the second time she called the store, she was able to confirm that the price was indeed $199. Great! Then she told me that they don't match in store prices. Not great! I had now been on the phone for way too long. What was the manager thinking? With three calls to the store to check price, and now they wouldn't honor the store price, why was I tied up on the phone with all of this checking?

Okay—now I needed the Call Center manager. My arguments—my extended time on the phone, the narrow time window in terms of purchase/receipt of package and further price reduction, and most importantly, the three time Hold to check the store price when there was no intention of honoring that price. The manager understood, and adjusted the price to the $199 store price.

What are the incentives to provide customer service and to honor legitimate pricing issues in a retail setting—as well as in many other settings in which there should be a concern for the customer base? The obvious major reason is that the company wants to retain customers. So, arguing that you will no longer be a customer if the issue is not satisfactorily resolved is a good move. Another reason for a business to properly resolve issues is to maintain a good public profile. As I've said before, word of mouth is a powerful advertising tool with the potential for positive as well as negative impact. Using this knowledge can help you to accomplish your goal. By being clear that business will be lost if the retailer doesn't

CUSTOMER SERVICE—THE INS AND OUTS

do the right thing, you can often have impact. I don't believe that the customer is always right, since I've seen some wild customer requests. But customer service should always be prime, especially when the customer is really right.

SHOWDOWN IN THE MEN'S DEPARTMENT

My sister is the queen of online shopping. Other than eBay, I usually prefer to go into a store and see and touch what I'm buying. But, life is complicated, and finding what you want at the price you want may require a little more hunting, both in the real world and in the cyber world.

Howard and I were in New York just before Thanksgiving, and found the perfect rain jacket in a department store. It wasn't on sale, but since it was perfect, we bought it. I hate paying full price, but sometimes you gotta do what you gotta do. We had the jacket shipped, and it arrived about five days after we purchased it. Flash forward to Thanksgiving, a week after the jacket arrived.

My sister counts on online bargains around Thanksgiving, and looking at this store's site, she found Howard's jacket at 40% off. This was a big price difference! Howard hadn't worn the jacket yet—he hadn't even taken off the tags. Now, here I was, in front of the computer, with notification of a sale price, one week after the jacket had arrived. Logically, for the exact same item, from the same retailer, I should be able to get a price adjustment, given the small window of time between purchase date/jacket arrival and the date of the online sale. I printed the online pricing page with the date on it, and the Saturday after Thanksgiving, walked into my local branch with my receipt

CUSTOMER SERVICE—THE INS AND OUTS

and the printout. Not only was there an online sale, there was an in store sale, as well. The reasonable conclusion was that I would get a discounted price either way. I explained the issue, and thought that this would be an easy transaction.

Easy was not the word of the day. When I showed the printout and receipt to the salesman, he said that there was a seven day price adjustment policy. I pointed out several logical arguments. First, although the jacket had been purchased ten days before the price change, the jacket had arrived seven days prior to the printout date, so that I was technically within their adjustment time frame. However, regardless of whether he was looking at purchase date or date of arrival, given the narrow time differential, and the fact that the jacket hadn't been worn and still had the tags on it, this seven day issue seemed superfluous.

Of course, expecting better customer service, I hadn't brought the jacket with me, since it was more convenient to bring the papers, rather than to lug the jacket around. I've also had price adjustments in other stores, and they never required the item—only the receipt. The salesman suggested that I come back with the jacket to show the tags on it, and he could look into making an adjustment. Now, he's toast! Next argument—I pointed out that if I had to drive home and return with the jacket, it was very likely that I would return the jacket, buy it elsewhere, chalk the whole incident up to terrible customer service and cancel my charge account. If this store wasn't customer service oriented, I could shop in better stores.

The salesman then threw in the added obstacle that they would take back my jacket and sell me a new one at the lower price—if there was one available in Howard's size. Game over. At that point, I asked for a manager.

Planting myself like a tree in the middle of the department, I was unwilling to accept this salesman's lack of customer service skills. Finally, standing there and not moving, making my arguments to the manager, they made the adjustment. As a little jab, the salesman added that they were very proud of their policies. I looked at him as if he'd lost his mind—though I may have driven him to that point—and jabbed back: "You shouldn't be", I replied. "Policies are only guidelines, and customer service is the goal—and you haven't met the goal."

Unfortunately, this little adventure wasn't over. I got home and looked at the receipt (which I should have done in the store). They had adjusted to the store sale price at 30% off, rather than the online 40% discount. I should have noticed the two different sale prices. This still left me with an excessive price gap.

I returned to the store a few days later, receipts and printouts in hand. My old friend, the salesman, looked up and saw me, smiled nervously, and asked if he could help. Having butted heads a few days earlier, he was a little better than last time. But, when I showed him the adjustment difference, he said that they don't match online prices. This didn't make sense.

He found a different manager this time. She pointed out that while online and store fall under the same company umbrella, the online and retail operations are separate businesses, and the online sector might be able to obtain a better bulk price, and therefore, pass this on to the customer. I have heard this business model before. But, I don't care. Same larger company, same item. It didn't make sense that the store couldn't match the online price. I've had other stores match prices of competitors, so it didn't feel right that this store wouldn't match their own online price, even if they were separate businesses under the same name. I'd guess that they were still making money. Again—there's nothing wrong with making money; the object is to make money and still treat the customer fairly.

She resisted; I insisted. Finally, worn down, she asked if she could go upstairs and research further, and offered me a bottle of water. "That's fine. Thank you for the water, but if it takes long enough for me to drink a bottle of water, this isn't

CUSTOMER SERVICE—THE INS AND OUTS

going to be pretty". I also pointed out that if she couldn't fix the problem, I would need to have the name and number of the Regional Manager, so that I could contact that person to explain the problem and why I would no longer be their customer. She swallowed, smiled wanly, and proceeded upstairs.

As the time passed—about twenty minutes, which was ten minutes more than it should have taken—I grew more irritable. Nearby, a man was loudly complaining that this store has very poor customer service, he expected better treatment, and he was going to shop somewhere else where there was better customer service. Additional strategy—as my salesman stood by, I approached the man and said, "I don't mean to intrude, but if you are having a bad sales experience, I have a manager checking on something for me, and I'm getting the name of the Regional Manager. Would you like that information?" The salesman grabbed the man by the arm and led him away—anything to get the customer away from this lunatic lady who could start a revolution! This was an honest strategy. I wanted them to know that I was serious about addressing the problem. And why shouldn't this man have options for escalation and resolution? Here I was, working on my problem and his simultaneously, with the salesman desperately trying to extricate the irate customer from my rescue attempt.

The manager finally came back, and said that she had called to a higher level. (Where? If there was no resolution, you could be sure that I was going to find out who that higher level was.) She had received the answer that they couldn't match online prices. To her credit, however, she was trying to be creative, and said that she would, instead, give me a store gift card for $50. This could have been a reasonable option. But after we both put on our reading glasses to see the fine print on expiration date, we found that the expiration date was only a couple of weeks away. By this time, I was tired of shopping and wasn't anticipating shopping any more in the next few weeks. I thanked her, but told her that, given the expiration date, I preferred the charge credit. The store would still have my business since my card was their store credit card and couldn't be used elsewhere. She caved.

While I don't claim to understand the Corporate business structure for separating the store versus online segments of the business, the logical customer service response in a problematic situation would be to satisfy the customer if the request is reasonable.

I returned to the scene of the raincoat adventure at a later date, because they had a Friends and Family Day with 25% off of almost everything in the store. Nothing was within my budget for that day. But, I did notice that they had designer sunglasses at the 25% off price. I glanced, and found the beauties that I had recently purchased at another department store sitting right there on the display. (My sunglass addiction again.) I checked and double checked—yep—they were the same ones.

I went home and called the store where I originally purchased the sunglasses. I reached Monica, a manager who really understood customer service—as does most of the staff at that store. I told her that I had bought the sunglasses at full price, saw them for 25% off today, and really didn't want to return them and re-purchase from their competitor, because I like her store better. Without hesitating, she asked for my credit card number and told me to look for the credit for the difference on my next bill. Not only did I thank her for her excellent customer service, she thanked me for calling rather than simply returning and re-buying.

Retailers are not always set up to pummel their customers. And despite my stories about bad service, I've also had good experiences in these stores. There are many good businesses out there, and if you have a reasonable request and ask nicely, they will often do lovely things in the name of customer service.

CALL CENTERS—DON'T CALL US

One evening, I picked up our phone and had no dial tone. Navigating through a string of Call Center cartoon characters became a bigger problem than the lack of a dial tone.

Trying normal channels first, I used my cell phone to call the company Service number. Going through automated voice prompts for what seemed to be forever, I finally reported the problem. Three hours later, I called to check status. I got an automated voice telling me that they were committed to having my problem fixed within four days. (Remember, this isn't the first time that I had heard this response. Four days seems to be the standard for this company's service time frame.) I banged on the number for the various prompts and cursed at the automated voice. This didn't speed things up but I finally reached a representative. She told me that four days wasn't unreasonable. This certainly wasn't resolving the problem. I asked for a supervisor. I spent 25 minutes in a queue, waiting for a supervisor. What was I thinking? More importantly, what was the phone company thinking? Or, more likely, they weren't thinking. I finally hung up. (Lesson learned—don't wait on Hold for more than seven minutes. Why seven? It's a nice number and as good as any other.)

I called back to the Service number. Another bad rep explained that the four day lag time was due to snow across the state. There was no snow across the state, and definitely none in my area. When I told her that, she responded that all of the technicians were busy. Which is just another way of saying that the customer doesn't matter. I asked for a supervisor, told her about the 25 minute wait, and asked that I either be connected now or receive a call back. No available supervisor; no call back. At that point, I went to my escalated contacts within the company. They came through, and phone service was restored quickly.

A few days later, we found that the problem recurred. Was this revenge for my not having waited the four days for service? Nah—stuff happens. This time, when I reached a rep, and, as usual, asked for last name or ID for documentation, she actually told me that she didn't have a last name and wouldn't give an ID, but that her name would be on my account. Very reassuring. And, how does someone not have a last name? Was she Biblical—was I really speaking to Job, Adam, Eve, Moses? Although I asked for a supervisor and clearly asked not to be put into the queue, of course, she put me into the queue.

Again, messages for my escalated contacts. Before my best contact could reach me, I received a call from a supervisor, based on one of the messages that I had left. She spoke gibberish and told me that I needed a four hour window for service if they couldn't fix the problem from the outside. Four hours is never a reasonable time frame. I'm usually able to narrow the time frame through persistence and/or contacts. At any rate, she obviously didn't like me. I don't blame her, since I made it obvious that I wasn't interested in the Corporate policy line. I asked for her supervisor. She said that she didn't have a supervisor. (Was I now talking to God?) I asked who was above her. She said that Corporate is above her. Then, I re-phrased the question—"Who do you report to?" Aahah!—I got a name. Of course, I went above her to that person and had the problem fixed quickly.

Interesting side note—at the end of the day, I received a call from someone instructed to let me know that they were putting a $50 credit on my account because of the problem. That was nice, but as an added feature, she tried to sell me more services with the company. Why would she think that this was a good time to try to sell me service with a provider whose service was so bad that it warranted escalation and a courtesy credit? More Corporate policy overshadowing Call Center problems, I guess.

FOREIGN TERRITORY

When planning a vacation, there are steps you can take to make the vacation go smoothly. Calling your credit card companies and your bank to put a foreign travel notice on your credit and ATM cards is an important precaution. This should allow seamless use of the card when the notice is on record. It usually works, but on the last day of a vacation, when we decided to shop, it didn't work.

We were in Paris and went to the beautiful Galeries Lafayette for our final hurrah. The beauty of this last outing was that the store itself is gorgeous, especially the magnificent early 1900s stained glass dome. It hurts my neck every time, looking up to enjoy that magnificent view. The store also has a charming history. This was where Coco Chanel purchased hats to decorate for her first group of society ladies before she became a famous couturier. It was there, walking by the store, where Picasso spotted his lifelong muse, Marie Therese Walter. With these little occurrences, the course of fashion and art were changed forever. The shopping there is great fun, too.

Prior to shopping, we had been using one credit card for daily purchases with no problem. We switched cards for the anticipated department store purchases. Our first purchase went smoothly. However, when we made a more expensive purchase, the credit card was declined. We correctly assumed

CUSTOMER SERVICE—THE INS AND OUTS

that this was a security issue because of the dollar amount and two purchases in a short time at the same store.

Howard called the out of country number on the back of the credit card to identify himself, thinking he could resolve the problem easily. Not so fast. He answered all of the security questions, but the representative kept putting him on hold to consult with a supervisor, finally saying that she needed one at the highest level. This took a whopping half hour out of our last day of vacation. Yes, whopping—when you're on vacation, every minute counts.

Finally, they released the card. Although the store was very understanding, and the Sales staff knew that this sort of thing happens on foreign purchases, it was a little embarrassing. The salesperson offered us a glass of champagne while we were waiting. (It wasn't that big a purchase; the French can be very civilized in retail.)

Why was this decline unacceptable?

1. It should have been sufficient for Howard to answer the security questions and return to completing the purchase.

2. If a high level supervisor was necessary, he/she should have been readily available. After all, this was a Fraud/Security unit. If there is a protocol on that end, it should be seamless for the consumer.

3. While the credit card company provides a collect call number for out of country calls, they forget that most people use cell phones and those foreign minutes add up to significant cost.

4. The credit card company took precious and excessive time on that last vacation day. I have no problem with

being protected from fraud, but this interaction should have taken five minutes.

I decided to address the problem with the credit card company when I returned home. Although all of my pre-trip preparation had worked fine for other credit and ATM transactions, it didn't prevent problems with this card. Of course, I needed to address the problem. Why?

1. We deserved to be compensated for our lost time, embarrassment, and expensive phone call. I didn't think a credit of few hundred dollars was unreasonable.

2. More importantly, I needed to make sure that the credit card company recognized the issue and took steps to address their system problem and employee problem so that this wouldn't happen again. I needed to feel secure in order to use that card in the future.

Using my escalation protocol, I started through standard channels. When I spoke to a Customer Service representative and explained the problem, all he offered was an additional 5000 reward points. I wasn't going to waste time arguing with this first line person, so I went up the ladder to a supervisor. I explained why there should be a credit on my card as compensation for our issue. The supervisor initially hedged, but I insisted. She placed me on Hold to speak with someone above her and offered to add $100 to the 5000 points. I told her that this was nice, but still inadequate compensation. She made excuses for the problem, which told me that she didn't see the big picture. So, I just asked her to add the $100 credit and the points and decided to move upward.

I had already spent too much time just to get this far. If a supervisor doesn't understand, it's not worth wasting your time by arguing. I made sure to get her name and continued to go up the ladder. When you are at this point, you don't need someone (the supervisor) to act as an intermediary. Better to go upward yourself. *No one is more qualified to express your problem to the person in charge than you are.*

How did I get to the right person? As usual, I Googled the credit card company's Corporate headquarters. Because the card was issued by a bank with many business subsidiaries, it wasn't easy to find the escalation area. So, I played a little more online, changing the search words that I used—Executive, Headquarters, Corporate, etc. Finally, I saw someone else's complaint online. The complaint identified the Executive Vice President by name and included a phone number. I reached the EVP's assistant and told her I had a problem that wasn't resolving through normal channels, and before I cancelled my credit card, I wanted to see if I could reach someone who could assure me that the company would stand behind their customer. In other words, I laid out the problem and pointed to the consequence of lack of resolution. She got me to the Executive Inquiry Department pronto.

The Executive Inquiry contact understood the problem and immediately offered a $250 credit in addition to the original 5000 points and $100 credit. Most importantly, he took all of the names and Call Center locations of the people we dealt with, from the contacts in Fraud/Security while we were away, to the Customer Service contacts on that last call when we returned. Armed with this information, he could trace the problem to the guilty parties and defective Call Centers. A week later he called and told me that the algorithm for our card had been adjusted so this shouldn't happen again, though he still made sure to keep us protected. He also addressed all of the individuals involved, using training and development staff to work on the Customer Service problem and create consumer friendly changes to the security system. I saved his contact information just in case I need it in the future. *When you have information for good contacts which could impact on vacation or work related travel, keep this information with you when you travel.*

The win for me was resolution and compensation; the win for the company was that the Executive Department's excellent service kept me from cancelling the card.

After this adventure, I needed another vacation!

Healthcare—The Challenges of Dealing with a World of Its Own

Although healthcare problems can often be resolved using the same principles that run through all of the issues in this book, healthcare does have constraints that are very specific to the industry. Having worked as a consumer advocate in healthcare for many years, I have become well aware that the industry operates within its own set of rules. And now, The Affordable Care Act is in place. Although The Affordable Care Act has some points that are very consumer oriented, it also misses the details and nuance that contribute to consumer problems. The broader pieces are logical and important—universal health insurance options, no penalty for pre-existing conditions, independent reviews of services denied for medical reasons. However, the act fails to consider that the nitty gritty day to day problems are breaking the system—claims that are processed incorrectly, services that are denied incorrectly, rules that are not clearly known to consumers.

HEALTHCARE—THE CHALLENGES

This doesn't mean that the whole system is evil—it's not. There are people who work in the health insurance industry who truly care about delivering good service to their members. But there are also some people in the industry who are problematic and who can create big problems. Generally, when there is a breakdown in service, the staff who create the problems are usually just linear. They have difficulty thinking in real world terms, having internalized a rigid system rather than a worldview. This isn't much consolation, but it can help a little to control the angst when you are in the middle of a problem. When you run into this scenario, you can still use the strategies that I've used in other industries to solve problems. Let's take a look at just a few.

A short history lesson—In the pre-managed care days—long, long ago—patients saw local physicians, who referred to specialists as needed. Generally, people had family physicians in their home area, and pretty much stayed with these doctors for most of their lives. Insurance companies existed, but they mainly paid claims. There were no referrals, no pre-certifications, fewer complicated rules and fewer policies that didn't make sense. It is important to remember that life was simpler in general back then, too, as were medical technology and healthcare delivery. The cost of medical care was not at the same level that it is today. As medical technology and medical care strategies have advanced, costs increased. The movement to find ways to control costs began. The result was the Managed Care system. It started with HMOs (Health Maintenance Organizations) that required the family physician to become a "gatekeeper" to control access to specialty care. Treatment was only covered when patients sought care from physicians and hospitals that were contracted with their insurance network. As the business models became more sophisticated, new "products" came along—PPOs (Preferred Provider Organization where there is an out of network benefit and generally no referral requirement), EPOs (Exclusive

Provider Organization which is like a PPO with a restricted network), and a slew of other business products. The operant word here is "business". The business models imposed by the insurance companies controlled the practice of medicine. The result was the development of an administratively bloated system, in which rules and protocols can be confusing and often override common sense. And, this system is costly—the administrative overhead required to administer benefits (claims, appeals, systems, rules, etc.) is staggering. At the same time, we have become a society of "I want what I want", so that consumers sometimes have unreasonable demands, as well. I'm simply trying to be fair here—while I see the bulk of the problem lying on the insurance end, I have to say that there are times when I see consumers with unrealistic expectations. The key to resolving the bigger problems in healthcare is balancing the system. And I really don't know how to do that on a broader level, although I have some ideas. The Federal or State governments haven't figured it out yet, either, although they do try.

There are some trends that I do see. With an emphasis on Wellness (Preventative services, such as colonoscopies, mammograms, and other testing for early detection and treatment of diseases that could become more difficult to treat if not found early), I often see situations in which claims are mishandled. For example, I frequently see people who undergo colonoscopies as Routine Screening. However, when a finding, such as a polyp, occurs, the protocol for billing is to bill with a diagnosis that includes the finding. Without a finding, the procedure would be billed with a Routine code. These claims autoadjudicate. (Don't you love the fact that there is an industry word for this piece of bureaucracy?) This means that they go through a computer system, without benefit of human touch, and because of this, the procedure is no longer viewed as Routine since it was billed with a non-routine diagnosis. The coverage protocol changes and the patient is charged more

HEALTHCARE—THE CHALLENGES

than if this would have autoadjudicated under the Wellness benefit. Then the fighting begins.

How do you fix it? When the service is processed incorrectly (so that it isn't covered, or is covered with too much charged to the patient), the patient will receive an Explanation of Benefits that should have a description stating why the claim paid as it did. It should also have instructions for appealing. Read carefully, since appeals have deadlines. The best way to appeal is to write a letter describing the fact that the service *intent* was Routine, and that the objective of this Routine service was early detection, which is exactly what occurred. Make sure that you obtain documentation from the facility where the procedure occurred, or, from your doctor. That documentation could be a chart note that states the order for a "Routine Colonoscopy", a prescription that says "Routine Colonoscopy" and/or a procedure report that says that the Admission Diagnosis was "Routine Colonoscopy".

When you submit the appeal, make sure that you mail it with some type of tracking, and call the Member Services number on your insurance card to verify that the appeal is on record. When you make that call, ask for the usual documentation—note the name of the representative to whom you speak with last name, initial or employee ID number and Call Center location. And, note the date of receipt of the appeal in the Appeals area. This is important, because, too often, I have heard the insurer say that they never received an appeal. For large corporations, most correspondence goes to a central mail area, and is then distributed to the appropriate department—or, sometimes not. If you have specific documentation of your letter, then you have some leverage if there is a problem.

Another problem—Emergency Room visits. If you've had a cold for a week, and decide at 4 PM today that you can't stand it any more but can't make a doctor's appointment until tomorrow, that's not a good reason to go to the Emergency Room. Unless there is a dire and immediate concern where you feel that you are in serious jeopardy, where possible, it is probably best to call your doctor's office about going to the Emergency Room. Most doctors' offices have after hours on call physicians if you are calling outside of normal business hours. But, in the final analysis, if you feel that you are at risk of a major medical problem, you need to do what you need to do to access care asap.

I have seen many Emergency Room visits denied because the presenting issue turned out not to be a life threatening condition. However, most insurance contracts have language defining an Emergency as a situation in which a "prudent layperson" (someone without medical training) would believe that he/she is in jeopardy of serious illness or injury. *So, the argument on this issue would be that the incoming symptoms rather than the final diagnosis should dictate the coverage.* Even if your chest pain turns out to be heartburn, it isn't unreasonable for you to believe that your symptoms might have been life threatening. If you have to appeal a denial of Emergency Room services, it's always important to include medical records.

Sometimes, if the negative outcome isn't overturned on the first appeal, there can be a second appeal, which is sometimes a hearing. Hearings can be very powerful. The opportunity to present an argument to a panel (mostly on the phone, sometimes in person) can have significant impact based on visual and verbal presentation.

I worked with a client who was appealing the denial of coverage for an out of network eye specialist. She had a prosthetic eye. She had difficulty with fit, and the in network specialist hadn't been able to resolve it over an extended period of time. There was an out of network specialist who could take care of the problem, but the insurer refused to cover his service, taking the position that there were in network resources. Because her prosthetic eye was such an uncomfortable fit, she started wearing an eye patch. Then she decided to appeal the denial of the out of network services. She had documented the fit problems with chart notes, descriptions of the issue, and detail about the lack of appropriate in network resources.

The first level appeal upheld the denial. She was offered a hearing. Because this was held locally, we decided that it would be a good idea for her to go to the hearing. She brought both her old and new prosthetic eyes with her. The committee enjoyed playing with the two sets of eyes. She told them that she was used to this—her children also liked to play with them. With the live demonstration, the committee was able to see the difference in fit, recognized the network gap problem, and covered all charges related to the new eye.

In another situation, a consumer had chosen his primary care doctor, Dr. Jones. Dr. Jones was part of the "Medical Group of XX County". In the booklet that listed primary care doctors in his network, there was "Medical Group of XX County" and "THE Medical Group of XX County". The patient accidentally chose "THE Medical Group of XX County" as his primary care group, when he meant to choose "Medical Group of XX County". When he received a referral for specialist services, he found that the coverage was denied because he didn't have a referral from his primary care physician. Of course he had a proper referral. There was an understandable administrative snafu due to the similarity of the names of the two groups.

When the patient appealed, the denial was upheld. I helped him with the hearing. It's always important to read documents carefully. When I read the Level One denial letter, I found that they had misspelled the patient's name. They had misspelled the name of the specialist to whom he was referred. "Wow", I thought, "These are common mistakes". This was a really good argument in a hearing. I spent the hearing repeating that anyone can make a mistake, and quoted the errors in the letter, repeating my observation that "Medical Group of XX County" and "THE Medical Group of XX County" sound very similar—ad nauseam. Finally, the committee gave up. "We get it", the committee chair said. We won.

THE CASE OF THE DEAD DOCTOR

On a snowy day, Jimmy decided to go sledding. He fell off of the sled and hurt his arm. His father took him to their family doctor. The doctor looked at the arm and told Dad that Jimmy needed an x-ray. Dad's insurance plan required a referral in order to cover the x-ray charge. The doctor gave him a note on a prescription pad saying "X-ray at XYZ Hospital". Dad's doctor participated in his network, so he trusted that the doctor was following the rules by handing him this referral. He was told to take Jimmy to the hospital, and he had a piece of paper referring him to the hospital

The good news was that Jimmy's arm wasn't broken. The bad news was that Dad received an Explanation of Benefits from his insurance company saying that his plan required a referral from his primary care doctor for the x-ray, there was no referral, and he was responsible for the bill. Dad didn't understand how the insurance company could say that he didn't have a referral, when he had that little piece of paper in his hand.

He called the insurance company. They told him that they didn't have a referral on file. He faxed them a copy of his little paper referral. They told him that this wasn't a referral. He was confused. If this paper was on the doctor's prescription paper, told him to go to a specific hospital, and told him to get the x-ray, how could this not be considered a referral? The Customer Service representative couldn't explain it.

Dad called me to try to get this fixed. I could see immediately that Dad had attempted to follow the rules using this paper referring Jimmy for the x-ray. However, what Dad didn't know was that a referral is a formal process. It is generally transmitted electronically from one medical office (in this case, his family doctor's office) to another medical office (the hospital x-ray department). There is a piece of paper that can be generated, but it is pretty much a form, with detail like numbers representing the medical offices, medical codes, etc.

The informal piece of paper reminded me of an old joke—Lady goes up to a hotel doorman and says: "Call me a cab". Doorman says: "You're a cab". Dad may have thought he had a referral, but in reality, this referral wasn't any more real than the joke lady's cab.

Dad had thought that everything was in order. The hospital should have known that he needed a formal referral, so it was unclear why they didn't get involved before the x-ray was done. The doctor's office should have known about referrals, so it's unclear why they didn't put a formal referral through the system. With all of this said, with so many insurance plans with different protocols, situations like this can fall through the cracks.

I represented Dad in a hearing with the insurance company to try to get the bill paid by the insurer. First, I needed to understand why the doctor hadn't done a formal referral. I called the doctor's office. Sadly, I found that the doctor had died. Now, I didn't have an eyewitness to defend Dad's action.

What could I do? I could explain to the Appeals hearing committee that Dad had followed every logical step to obtain a referral—he went to his family doctor and he had obtained a referral. How was he to know that this scrap of paper wasn't a formal referral? Jimmy had the x-ray, which was the medically appropriate step, so he shouldn't be denied coverage of appropriate medical care based on an unintentional administrative snafu. My intention was to say that, unfortunately, I wasn't able to understand the doctor's reasoning because he had since passed away. My plan was to make the committee understand that intent of the rule was honored, but the detail got a little confused through no fault on Dad's part. But, I couldn't explain further because the eyewitness (the doctor) couldn't be at the hearing to explain because he was now deceased. Dad now knows that he needs a formal referral for future service, and based on all of this, the bill should be covered. *A very brief, logical argument—substance over bureaucracy.*

I started out fine. But, before I could mention the doctor's death, the committee jumped in first and asked why the doctor hadn't done a proper referral. In my zeal to underscore that we couldn't clarify why this happened, instead of quietly saying that the doctor had passed away, as I had intended to say, the words "BECAUSE HE'S **DEAD!**" fell out of my mouth. The hearing was conducted over the telephone, so I couldn't see faces, but I could hear stunned silence. What do I do now?

I quickly recovered my composure and returned to my professional voice. Fortunately, no one saw my horror stricken face—one of the great benefits of telephonic communication. We won.

How did I do it?

1. I argued that the intent of the rule had been fulfilled.

2. I pointed out that the chicken scratch on a prescription pad looked like a referral to the layman's eye.

3. The element of unplanned surprise ("BECAUSE HE'S **DEAD**") probably helped. (This is not my typical strategy.)

4. We also added that, now that Dad knows what a referral is supposed to look like, he will know for the future.

If you can demonstrate a reasonable explanation as to why a rule wasn't formally followed, the fact that the situation that took place was an appropriate one, and you do understand the rule for future reference, you can sometimes win your argument. The sad and frustrating factor is that outcome often depends on the players and the company—erratic and no guarantees.

HIDDEN PROVIDERS

Mr. Jones had a minor procedure performed as an outpatient in a hospital. He did his due diligence before the procedure. He made sure that the doctor and the hospital were in his network. He expected to pay his copay with no other charges. He was surprised when he received a bill for $850 from an anesthesiologist—someone he hadn't known about.

This is a common scenario—"hidden providers" in what appears to be a network situation. Frequently, captive services (neonatologists, emergency room doctors, anesthesiologists, pathologists, radiologists, and others) can provide services in a network facility, but these clinicians have chosen not to participate in the insurance networks with which the hospital participates. (Sidebar—I hate the term "provider"—it takes away the professional status of a clinician.) In these "hidden provider" situations, it's hard to tell the good guys from the bad guys. Clinicians in this situation usually feel that insurance reimbursement is too low, and knowing that they will have business because of the hospital setting, they don't participate with insurance. And I've seen reimbursement rates all over the map. In one lab situation where the claim was denied, the charge was $800. The lab agreed to charge the patient $500 if the insurance wouldn't pay the claim. On appeal, I was able to obtain coverage. The lab was in network with the insurance company, and accepted the insurance amount as payment in full—$87.26. Broken system—the cost of appealing was far more than the cost of the service, and the gap in the various numbers was—I don't know—pick a term—silly, mindboggling, bureaucratic, greedy, stingy—whatever.

For "hidden provider" situations, patients often don't even know that these people are involved in their care until they receive the bill, or, in some situations, they believe that the doctors are part of the network because the hospital is in network. It can turn ugly, because these clinicians can bill the patients for charges over what insurance pays, even if the claims are processed at the in network rate. Some contracts have provisions for in network coverage in these situations, which usually means that they pay the in network allowance, which is usually much lower than the charges, though once in a while, insurance will pay full charges. It's very difficult to anticipate these situations. But, a few things that you can do:

1. If you are seeing a doctor or having a procedure where there could be hidden services—lab charges, anesthesia, radiology, assistant surgeons, etc., it would be best to talk to your in network doctor or hospital to find out if these services might be a part of your care.

2. If you find that there will be additional services that are not within your network, talk to the "hidden" service provider's office to see if they would be willing to reduce charges up front

3. Ask the doctor or the hospital (Patient Advocate, Administrative office) if they could talk to the other provider(s) on your behalf about reduction in charges or see if there are any other specialists in the hospital who do participate in your network so that you can use those services instead of the out of network services.

4. The best option, if possible, would be to call your insurance company before the procedure and explain that you have no choice and see if they can agree to cover the service(s) at the in network benefit and possibly to full charges, or whether they would negotiate with the clinician's office up front. Sometimes they will and sometimes they won't.

I assisted a client whose child required a long stay in a newborn intensive care unit. The neonatologist wasn't in the family's insurance network and the charges really added up. I attempted to appeal the level of reimbursement, but wasn't successful, since this contract didn't provide for higher coverage. I then tried to negotiate with the doctor's billing service. They didn't have the power to negotiate, so I went to the doctor's clinical office. They wouldn't negotiate. I decided to try to go through the hospital. While the doctor was not employed by the hospital and was therefore an independent entity, I thought that the hospital administration could have some clout, based on the fact that this situation was occurring in their facility, and a high charge wouldn't be a good reflection on the hospital, even if the problem was the doctor's bill and not a hospital issue.

I went on the hospital's website to find the names and phone numbers for Executive staff. I noticed the hospital's mission statement, which included the commitment to compassion and charity. I reached an administrative assistant in the CEO's office, explained the situation, and pointed out that the problem conflicted with the mission statement, being neither compassionate nor charitable. This started a move towards negotiation. The hospital acted as intermediary with the doctor. Finally the insurer and doctor negotiated a reasonable solution so that the family was taken out of financial harm's way.

These are just a few of the pitfalls of the current healthcare system. Often, a patient, hospital or doctor's office does everything that should be done, and problems still occur. It's important to read your benefit handbook so that you know how your benefit works. While it isn't an exciting read, you need to take some personal responsibility and familiarize yourself with the terms of your plan. If you don't find the answer to your question, or if you are confused, call the insurer's Member Service Department. That number is usually on the back of your insurance card. Ask your question, and if you aren't getting an answer that makes sense, ask for a supervisor. As always, make sure that you note the date that you call and get the names of the people you talk to, with the usual specifics. Frequently, there is a call reference number. Armed with this information, if there is a problem later, you will be able to reference the call. Many insurers record the calls, though they may or may not be able to listen at a later date. They should be able to at least see a note about the call. While this armament doesn't guarantee that the problem will be fixed, it can help and sometimes it does resolve the issue. And, most insurance companies have Executive Inquiry areas—the department name can vary, but if you Google the insurer, you can usually find an executive name, and can get to someone in an escalated area to help you.

Never be afraid to ask questions—lack of knowledge is pretty much a guarantee of a problem.

MAXIMIZING YOUR INSURANCE COVERAGE

"I pay for my insurance and now they won't pay for my treatment!"

"I'm healthy and never use my insurance but when I need it, they won't pay!"

These are just a few comments that I hear when people seek treatment and find that the treatment is not covered by their insurance. A common reason is that it doesn't meet Medical Necessity criteria. People often ask how the insurer can say that a medical intervention isn't necessary when their doctor knows their medical condition and makes a treatment decision based on the doctor's experience and the patient's situation.

Medical Necessity is an insurance industry term used by every medical insurer. The broad definition is that the service must be required and appropriate for diagnosis and treatment of a covered medical condition and must meet recognized professional standards. This seems pretty straightforward and clear. But, it's not always so clear. And when it gets murky, the battles begin.

How can you know if a treatment meets Medical Necessity standards? All insurers use written clinical guidelines for assessment of most treatment interventions. Many have the guidelines listed on their websites. You can usually find them by Googling "clinical policy" along with the name of your insurance company, which will lead you into the website to locate their treatment guidelines. Sometimes, the insurer uses guidelines that are published by a third party. Either way, if coverage is denied, patients are entitled by law to access to the documents used to make an adverse determination.

How can you maximize your chances of having services covered?

1. In many cases, a pre-certification is required prior to obtaining the service. In this situation, the doctor's office calls the insurance company and provides clinical information. The insurer uses that information to decide whether or not the service will be covered. If you have a pre-certification up front, you will usually know that you have coverage.

2. If a pre-certification is not required, you can have your doctor, therapist, or other professional look at the guidelines to see if you meet the criteria. But, "no pre-certification required" simply means what it says—that pre-certification isn't required, not that it's automatically covered.

Armed with this information, you will at least have some idea about whether or not you are going to have a coverage problem. But, it's not foolproof. Remember, what is certified upfront has to be the same as what is billed after the fact so that they match up. If there is an extenuating situation that creates a change—for example, surgery is approved, but something occurs during the surgery to alter the procedure—it's a good idea for the medical documentation to go with the claim to the insurer, so that the insurer can understand what happened and hopefully, cover the surgery regardless of the change. Sometimes, it's helpful for the doctor to speak with the medical review area at the insurance company to elaborate, and hopefully obtain coverage.

What if you don't fit neatly into the criteria? My father was a physician, and he often talked about the fact that the practice of medicine is part science and part art. How very true! We are not a nation of perfectly round pegs that always fit into perfectly round holes. I have been fortunate in dealing with insurance company medical directors who were smart and compassionate, and who understood the complexity of patient needs. On the other hand, there are physicians who haven't seen a patient in years and have the luxury of sitting in a remote office, making decisions that make life hell for the patients and treating physicians who live in the real world. It wouldn't be a bad idea for insurance staff to spend some time every year in the patient care world. Let them see how difficult it is in the trenches. Unfortunately, that's not part of the Affordable Care Act. Maybe it should be.

But for now, what can be done when services are denied?

1. On the physician end, doctors can usually speak with insurance company medical directors to see if they can convince the medical director that the service should be covered. I know of several physicians who have told the denying medical directors that they will document medical director names in the patient charts. Most medical directors don't like that, preferring to remain hidden. But, *power without responsibility and accountability isn't acceptable,* so naming names isn't a bad idea. Although this strategy is interesting and can be helpful, the best strategy is for the doctor to review the insurer's criteria and to be clear about how the patient status meets criteria for the specific intervention.

2. If you are appealing the denial of coverage, the best argument, where possible, is to draw a simple and direct line from Point A to Point B. In other words, look at the criteria that were used in the denial, and point by point, document how you met criteria. Medical records are critical in this process, and often, the treating clinician can write a letter that supports the argument for coverage by coordinating your medical condition with the insurance coverage guidelines.

3. If you don't fit neatly into the criteria, document where you do fit, and the extenuating circumstances that support the treatment. These are the most difficult situations to address, but I have frequently found that denials can be overturned on appeal review. For Medical Necessity decisions, if you aren't getting the overturn on the appeals to the insurer, most contracts have an appeal to a neutral third party external reviewer or to the Department of Insurance. I have seen some of those reviews uphold denials, but I have also seen some enlightened reviewers who view the medical situation more broadly and order coverage.

As in any consumer situation, push until there is nowhere else to go. I have worked on behalf of many people who fell into the "Not Medically Necessary" category, where there were extenuating circumstances or where the real facts were ignored.

I worked with a woman who had breast surgery a few years after having post-mastectomy breast reconstruction following a diagnosis of breast cancer. The insurer denied the coverage, saying that it was "Cosmetic", and therefore, didn't meet Medical Necessity criteria. Was it "Cosmetic"? Mostly. While she had discomfort in performing some activities because of the reconstruction, there was also a cosmetic aspect to the problem. The reviewer neglected to consider pain that impaired her ability to function fully. ("Functional Impairment" in insurance language). More importantly, he failed to consider Federal law. WHCRA, the Women's Health and Cancer Rights Act, is a legal mandate which has many provisions that guarantee certain rights to women who have had breast cancer, including surgery to correct problems related to mastectomy. With every denial on this case, I was increasingly floored to find that each reviewer ignored the law and cited lack of Medical Necessity to deny coverage, saying that there was not a functional impairment. If they read the records, they would have seen that there was a functional impairment. Although they declared that this was a cosmetic procedure (which was mostly true), they missed the fact that the procedure was covered based on WHCRA. I was sure that it would be a slam/dunk when the external review company reviewed the case. They blew it, too. Although she was entitled to one external review, I sent the review back six (yes, six) times, until I managed to finally have the surgery covered.

A 67 year old man had a denial of varicose vein surgery. Coverage was denied, with the "Cosmetic" rationale. The reviewers came to that conclusion based on the fact that he was missing one test measurement from the criteria. This type of situation gets funky, because here was a man who didn't go to the doctor often enough to have developed a significant trail of records. But when he finally needed surgery, he had significant symptoms to warrant this intervention. He had tried other options—medication, elevating his legs, support hose—all of the pre-surgery insurance requirement and all without relief. By the time his doctor decided that he needed surgery, he was having difficulty walking, standing and participating in normal activities. After reviews by the insurance company, he moved on to the external review. The reviewer for the external review agreed that this was "Cosmetic", mostly because he had his own philosophy about this type of surgery. Despite the fact that it was covered under specific conditions, this reviewer wrote a little treatise on why he didn't believe that this was a good surgical intervention in general. This wasn't the issue posed to him. So he, too, dumped it into the "Cosmetic" category. (I asked the client if he was planning to enter any beauty pageants, as a 67 year old male. Guess what his answer was.) Finally, after sending back for re-review (again, more than the mandated one review), I made my case, and obtained coverage for him. For one leg! This just shows how quirky and unpredictable our health care system has become.

The other common category used in denying coverage based on lack of Medical Necessity is "Experimental and Investigational". It sounds like an old time horror movie. The mad genius is doing weird experiments –like transplanting an ape's brain into a human. No, the insurance world isn't playing horror movie—it just feels like it when you get that denial. "Experimental and Investigational" simply means that the insurer's medical staff have reviewed findings and don't believe that it meets the required standard of care, or, that the treatment is proven, but not for the specific reason for which the patient is seeking treatment. I often hear "But it's FDA approved". Even when a treatment or test is FDA approved, some insurers believe that it hasn't been in use long enough to have substantial research support or hasn't been shown to be consistently effective.

As with "Not Medically Necessary", documentation and extenuating circumstances are keys to making an argument for coverage.

This all sounds evil. Sometimes it is and sometimes it isn't. There are times when the insurance companies are right. It's just that there are often debatable issues. If your doctor can make a reasonable argument, go for it. But, read the guidelines and coordinate with the insurer in order to make an informed decision about treatment. Sometimes it works, and sometimes it doesn't. But it's your best shot.

All too frequently, I run into misinformation problems. A patient calls the insurance company's Member Services number, and asks if a particular service is covered. The representative says that it is covered. The patient has the service, but finds that coverage is denied after the service is performed. This is where it is really important to document call detail—again, the usual—the date that you call, the time of day, the name of the representative with last name/initial/employee ID number. I often find that the representative either simply gave incorrect information, didn't bother to check detail carefully before giving information, or wasn't in a position to access the detail necessary for a correct response. If you simply ask, "Is XX treatment covered for XXX condition?" you may not receive a complete answer. The treatment may not be excluded from coverage, but the representative would not generally look at the medical necessity criteria. However, in that situation, he/she should at least make the disclaimer, "as long as you meet criteria" and then direct you to resources to obtain the criteria. *So, there is a need to take some personal responsibility. You need to have as much information as possible, and communicate it to the insurer, so that you can maximize your chance of receiving a complete and accurate answer. And if you're not sure that you're on firm ground, keep asking questions, going up the ladder if necessary.*

Most insurers (and some non-medical corporations) keep documentation of customer calls in computer systems or have access to recordings of calls. However, I have seen many situations in which the call records support the patient but the insurer continues to deny coverage, using the disclaimer that information quoted isn't a guarantee of coverage. This happens frequently, but as far as I'm concerned, that's bullfeathers! Unless you dropped your coverage, fell into some other major unredeemable situation, or didn't provide sufficient or accurate information for the representative to understand the question, the insurer should stand behind its member and cover services where information was disseminated incorrectly. After all, Customer Services Departments exist to provide information to members, in healthcare, as well as in other businesses. So if this is their mission, they should be responsible to get it right.

Fighting misinformation is difficult. You can go through the appeal process, but if you don't obtain coverage, go higher. The best way to do this is to make your way into escalated areas for Executive Inquiries. Google the Executive offices, and speak with someone there. Most insurers have dedicated teams to handle special circumstances such as these. On the other hand, some contacts are better than others. If you don't get the right answer, you may need to keep searching for the right contact. Sometimes that is someone else in the same area. I worked on a misinformation case where I made my way to an insurance company attorney, who reviewed all of the information and worked with the appropriate departments to have the service covered based on the misinformation given to the patient and to the doctor's office. This happened after I had exhausted many other staff resources. Depending on the type of contract you have, you may go to the Department of Insurance in the state where your contract was written or to your HR Department. But, keep going until there's nowhere else to go. And, hopefully, until you obtain the right answer.

There are also contract issues that determine whether or not a service is covered. While there are many appropriate treatments out there, they are not all covered under the insurance contract. This isn't evil; it's just the way contracts are written. Sometimes the insurer makes it a policy not to cover certain treatment; other times, the employer group chooses to add or delete coverage for certain services.

Hearing aids are usually excluded from coverage. Weight control surgery is often excluded from coverage, although there are some contracts that do cover it. Infertility services can be excluded or covered, but often have limitations. When a service is excluded from coverage, unless there has been misinformation from the insurer, don't waste your time chasing reimbursement. I worked with a woman who insisted that since her doctor said that a Tempurpedic bed would be therapeutic for her back problems, the insurer should cover it. All insurance policies have a restriction that states that equipment must be useful expressly for medical purposes and that equipment that can be used in non-medical situations isn't covered. I really couldn't help her; there wasn't an argument to support coverage. Yes, the bed may have been medically useful. But, it was equipment that wasn't used exclusively for the treatment of a medical problem. The last I heard, she was going to sue the insurer. I can guess what came of that.

Bottom line in figuring out your coverage and how to maximize reimbursement and minimize expenses:

1. Check your coverage—call Member Services and read your contract/Member Handbook. It may not be a fun read, but it's important.

2. Check the requirements for coverage so that you can make an informed decision.

3. If you think that you have an argument for coverage, as always, use your consumer skills to go as far as you have to go to get the right answer.

A FEW WORDS TO THE WISE

When people go on vacation, they often fail to consider that they might need to plan for an unexpected medical emergency. I do. Of course I do—I'm a pretty compulsive planner.

Generally, medical insurance plans cover emergency services anywhere that they occur—in or out of your home area. But, consider the fact that coverage doesn't mean paying for all costs. This is an important consideration, especially when you are far from home or out of the country. That is why travel medical insurance is a good idea. (*Senior Citizen Alert—* Medicare has restrictions, especially for foreign claims. So, for those of you who want to travel when you retire, remember that you really need extra coverage if you want peace of mind about possible emergencies.)

I have worked with people who have had wonderful vacation plans that turned into chaos—skiing accidents, injuries while on a cruise—all kinds of problems that can't be anticipated and that you hope won't happen to you. When they do happen, there are all kinds of costs that go beyond the normal insurance coverage.

Even in the United States, when you receive emergency services, not all of those services fall within your network. The emergency room doctors, the radiologist who reads your x-ray, the pathologist who looks at your lab tests, possibly even the hospital—any of these, and others, may not participate in your network. While some (and not always all) of these charges may pay at the network level of benefit, that only means that the insurance company has to pay what they would pay if the services were performed by an in network provider. Most often, this amount is not the same as the full charge. But we're talking vacation here. So, while it's always aggravating to incur unanticipated bills, when you're on vacation, you don't want to add aggravation. If you carry travel medical insurance, there are benefits that cover some or all of the costs beyond what your insurance will reimburse.

If you are traveling outside of the country, it can be more complicated. I worked with a man who was injured while on a cruise. He required medical transport from the cruise ship to land. Once he reached land, he was far from a hospital and required a long ambulance transport to a hospital. All of the services, including the hospital, required payment up front, providing a receipt to the patient for future insurance reimbursement. This is standard for medical treatment abroad. And, he wasn't in any condition to go back to the cruise, so he had to be transported home early, by air, along with his wife. While you still have to file claims through your insurance company first, if you have travel insurance, there are provisions for coverage of balances and additional services that usually aren't covered by your regular medical insurance plan, such as transport home with a companion. A ruined vacation and a medical problem are never good. But, if you purchase travel medical insurance, some of the headache goes away when you find that a significant portion of the services, if not all, are reimbursed. (And, there are travel policies that cover more than medical—flight delays, hotel problems, etc. Take a look at those, too.)

Another pretty obvious issue isn't so obvious to everyone, but it can cause real problems. If you change insurance plans, keep your old card from your prior coverage where you can find it in case you have a late problem with a claim under that prior coverage. But make sure to put the new card in your wallet immediately.

I have had clients who gave the wrong (old) insurance card to a doctor or hospital when they needed medical care. When an incorrect insurance is billed, all kinds of problems arise. If the timing is right, the claim may be paid. But, the insurer usually realizes that there was an error, and retracts the payment. Then the fun begins—getting the service re-billed to the correct insurer. Will the correct insurer just pay the claim? Maybe, but maybe not. They may require verification that the claim was billed on time in order to pay. Then you have to go back to the provider to obtain the copy of the original bill, or to the old insurer to have a copy of the Explanation of Benefits showing that the claim was billed within the timely filing range. (There is a limit to the length of time in which a claim can be submitted. That varies depending on the contract and who is submitting the bill.) Or, the insurer doesn't pay the claim and the patient is billed. I have had patients just pay the bill, thinking that it was what they owed (Deductible, Coinsurance) and realize long afterwards that the claim should have been billed to the correct insurer, but the card wasn't on file with the medical office or hospital, so it just went to the patient. These problems can take much time and angst to solve. So, just avoid the problem—when the card comes in the mail, it should go with you everywhere.

KEEPING THE MOMENTUM GOING

In the 1976 film, *Network*, actor Peter Finch plays anchorman Howard Beale, who has lost his job and views the world solely through his angst. His memorable words in response to this:

"I'M AS MAD AS HELL, AND I'M NOT GOING TO TAKE THIS ANYMORE!"

While I haven't reached Howard Beale's level of instability, he does have a point. But, rather than rant, I would rather do something. Issue by issue. (Yes, there are times when I rant, but as you can see, I also take action.)

You see how I've accomplished goals, righted wrongs and see wrongs that remain so that there is always a cause to address. Now, you have the toolbox to challenge what needs challenging. Do it and see what happens.

Spread the word—if more people challenge unreasonable situations, the world can become a more civilized place.

ACKNOWLEDGMENTS

Walking out of the movie theater after seeing *Julie and Julia*, Howard turned to me and said, "Julie had her recipe a day; you have your issue a day. Why don't you write a book?" He threw down the gauntlet. I had to rise to the challenge.

Thanks to Howard, the best husband in the world, for starting me on this journey and for accompanying me through it. His patience, living through the events with me, choosing a title, technical support—everything starts and ends with Howard.

Running a close second, John Elduff, publisher, JTE Multimedia, who guided me through the process of getting the book written and published. His support, knowledge and cheerleading were invaluable.

To my wonderful family, Cory, Tracy and Jonah, thanks for their fine tuned eyes and ears as they read and reviewed, listened to endless ideas and added their valuable input. And the same to my gracious and patient test readers—Judy Gewitz, Ellen Taupin, Elinor Hewitt and Bob Grim. Eternal thanks to Tom Schneider, whose sage and unique view of the world has added so much to my own worldview.

Collaboration with illustrator Paula Hewitt Amram was a great meeting of the minds and a fun adventure. I couldn't ask for a more talented artist to enhance this project.

My parents, George and Belle Kolander, started me on this path a long time ago. Their teaching by example and their forbearance in raising a consumer advocate put me on the route to this book.

Finally, to the cast of characters who populate my book and others who are out there, but didn't make it into the book—the good guys and the not so good guys. Thanks to the good guys for getting it right. To the not so good guys, take a lesson from the good ones and ramp it up. We need for you to do that so that we can live in a more civilized and consumer friendly world.

www.ingramcontent.com/pod-product-compliance
Lightning Source LLC
Chambersburg PA
CBHW051637170526
45167CB00001B/225